James J. Burshek SJ

The PSALMS for TODAY

Mark Link, s.j.

*Praying an old book
in a new way*

D0104933

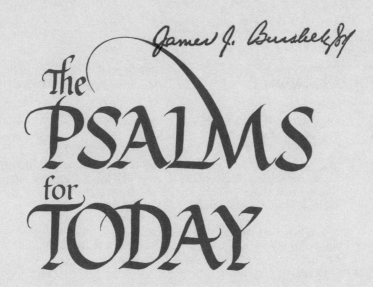

TABOR
PUBLISHING

Valencia, California   Allen, Texas

Imprimi Potest:
Robert A. Wild, S.J.

Nihil Obstat:
Msgr. Joseph Pollard, S.T.D., V.F.
Censor Deputatus

Imprimatur:
Most Rev. Roger M. Mahony, D.D.
Archbishop of Los Angeles

June 1, 1988

The *Nihil Obstat* and *Imprimatur* are official declarations that the work contains nothing contrary to Faith and Morals. It is not implied thereby that those granting the *Nihil Obstat* and *Imprimatur* agree with the contents, statements, or opinions expressed.

Unless otherwise noted, Scripture passages are taken from *The New American Bible with Revised New Testament* © 1970, 1986 by the Confraternity of Christian Doctrine, Washington, D.C. All rights reserved.

The English translation of the psalm responses are from the *Lectionary for Mass* © 1969, International Committee on English in the Liturgy, Inc. All rights reserved.

COVER ILLUSTRATION   Katherine Armstrong
CALLIGRAPHY   Bob Niles
INSIDE SPOT ILLUSTRATIONS   Debbie Allen

PHOTO CREDITS
David Daniel   18, 72, 90, 144
Mark Link   126
Chris Luneski/Image Cascade   36
Lisa Means   viii, 54, 108, 162, 180

Send all inquiries to:
Tabor Publishing
25115 Avenue Stanford, Suite 130
Valencia, California 91355

Printed in the United States of America

ISBN 0-89505-758-1

1 2 3 4 5   92 91 90 89 88

Contents

About This Book

Symphony conductor Guy Harrison had a notebook in which he summarized every book he had ever read. "Rereading these notes," he said, "allowed me to recapture the spirit and substance of each book."

What Harrison's notebook did for him, the psalms did for Israel. They summarized in prayer form the "spirit and substance" of the Old Testament. This explains why Old Testament readings in many worship services are followed by the reading of a psalm. This psalm is often referred to as a responsorial psalm, because its reading is usually punctuated by responses from the congregation.

The responsorial psalms are excerpted versions of the original psalms, which would often be too long to be read or sung in their entirety.

When the author decided to put together *The Psalms for Today,* he had two reasons for basing it on the responsorial psalms.

First, this is the way the average congregation hears the psalms at worship services. Thus, their hearing of these psalms would be enriched and enhanced.

Second, the abbreviated responsorial psalms make for a simpler introduction to the psalms for the average person.

How to Use This Book

There are three ways you can use *The Psalms for Today*.

First, you can read it as you would read any other book on a subject you want to learn more about.

Second, you can use it for "mood" reading. That is, you can keep it handy for those times when you want to read something that fits a certain mood or situation you are in—for example, when you are sick, grief-stricken, lonely, overwhelmed with joy. Some suggestions for mood reading are listed in Appendix A.

Finally, you can use it for daily meditation. Simply take one "meditation page" a day and reflect on it. These pages always include the same four elements:

1. *The liturgical response*
2. *The Old Testament psalm*
3. *A New Testament application*
4. *A personal application*

Reflect on each of these elements, using the following steps: *Read* it slowly. *Ponder* it prayerfully. *Speak* to God about it. *Listen* to what God may wish to say to you about it. End your meditation by rereading the psalm slowly.

An ideal setting in which to use *The Psalms for Today* is with a small group of six to eight people. The group should meet weekly for support and sharing.

Each chapter contains material for two weeks of meditation. A guide for personal reflection or group discussion for each week is provided at the end of each chapter.

What Are the Psalms?

1 *The Book of Psalms
is not a collection of prayers,
but a school of prayer.*

Anonymous

Imagine you are walking barefoot along the seashore. Feel the crunch of the sand beneath your feet. Listen to the music of the surf. The sand and the sea are as old as time. But they can also be as new as the footprints of two lovers walking along a beach. It all depends on how you approach them.

The Book of Psalms is much the same. It is old, like the sea and the sand. But it can also be as new and as fresh as the dawning of a new day. It all depends on how you approach it.

The Book of Psalms was Israel's meditation book. It expressed in prayer the history, beliefs, and feelings of God's people. Thus, more than any other book of the Bible, it lets us glimpse the "soul" of God's people. We see how they prayed in times of deep doubt, depression, and joy.

The Book of Psalms was also Israel's songbook. God's people were an emotional people; they expressed their total being in prayer. "To sing is to pray twice," they believed.

To catch the spirit in which the Israelites sang or prayed the psalms, imagine three settings.

The first is under the open stars at night. Picture a group of people around a campfire. Suddenly someone begins strumming a musical instrument. Conversation stops, and the people begin to sing. The psalms were a form of entertainment, as the people relaxed at the end of a hard day's work in the fields.

A second setting in which the psalms were sung was in the Temple on holidays and on the Sabbath. One way this was done was by alternating between the congregation and the choir, much as many modern Christians recite or sing the responsorial psalms in their worship services. Drums and trumpets often enhanced the dialogue.

A final setting in which the psalms were prayed was by an individual, alone. Picture a father sitting outside his house after his family has gone to bed. He looks up at the stars and recites from memory:

> *When I behold your heavens,*
> * the work of your fingers,*
> * the moon and the stars which you set in place—*
> *What is man that you should be mindful of him,*
> * or the son of man that you should care for him?*
> Psalm 8:4–5

The father then pauses and meditates. He ends his meditation by speaking to God in his own words, much as Tevye in the play *Fiddler on the Roof* used to speak to God in his own words.

It is in this third setting that you will be using this book: reading, meditating, and communing with God.

You are now ready to begin. As you do, remember that you are praying the same psalms that Jesus prayed in his lifetime.

Happy are they who hope in the Lord.

The play *Teahouse of the August Moon* opens with Sakini walking to the footlights, bowing to the audience, and introducing the play that is to follow. The Book of Psalms opens in a similar way. The psalmist introduces his work, saying:

*Happy the man who follows not
   the counsel of the wicked
     Nor walks in the way of sinners,
  nor sits in the company of the insolent,
But delights in the law of the LORD
   and meditates on his law day and night.*

*He is like a tree
   planted near running water,
That yields its fruit in due season,
   and whose leaves never fade.
[Whatever he does, prospers.]*

*Not so the wicked, not so;
   they are like chaff which the wind drives away.
For the LORD watches over the way of the just,
   but the way of the wicked vanishes.*   (1–4, 6)

Jesus may have had this psalm in mind when he said, "A tree is known by its fruit." *Matthew 12:33* Or again when he said, "Every tree that does not produce good fruit will be cut down and thrown into the fire." *Luke 3:9*

What kind of fruit is your life bearing at this moment? What fruit are you most proud of? Least proud of? Speak to Jesus about how your life can become even more fruitful.

Happy are all
who put their trust in the Lord.

When Israel anointed a king, he became God's "son" in a special sense. To conspire against the king was to conspire against God. It was sheer folly.

Why do the nations rage
and the peoples utter folly?
The kings of the earth rise up,
and the princes conspire together
against the Lord and against his anointed:
"Let us break their fetters
and cast their bonds from us!"

He who is throned in heaven laughs;
the Lord derides them.
Then in anger he speaks to them;
he terrifies them in his wrath:
"I myself have set up my king
on Zion, my holy mountain."

I will proclaim the decree of the Lord:
The Lord said to me, "You are my son;
this day I have begotten you.
Ask of me and I will give you
the nations for an inheritance
and the ends of the earth for your possession.
You shall rule them with an iron rod;
you shall shatter them like an earthen dish!"   (1–9)

Jesus is the King of Kings toward whom all of Israel's other kings pointed. He is God's true Son.

Speak to Jesus about how you can best serve him in his work of bringing to completion God's kingdom on earth.

Day three   Psalm 3

Lord, rise up and save me.

There are times in life when storm clouds block out the sun and everything turns dark. Nothing is right. Even our friends seem to be against us. Fear and worry grip our heart and hold us hostage. The psalmist knew times like this. When they came upon him, he turned to God's "holy mountain" and prayed:

O Lord, how many are my adversaries!
Many rise up against me!
Many are saying of me,
"There is no salvation for him in God."

But you, O Lord, are my shield;
my glory, you lift up my head!
When I call out to the Lord,
he answers me from his holy mountain.

When I lie down in sleep,
I wake again, for the Lord sustains me.
I fear not the myriads of people
arrayed against me on every side.
Rise up, O Lord!
Save me, my God!   (2–8)

Jesus may have recalled this psalm when his own disciples deserted him and he stood alone before the mob in the Garden of Gethsemane.   (Mark 14:50)

Picture Jesus in the garden, hemmed in on every side by foes brandishing torches and clubs. Listen to Jesus as he lies in a dungeon later that night, praying aloud Psalm 3. Share your feelings with Jesus.

5

Day four   Psalm **4**

Lord, let your face shine on us.

Lecturer David Hubbard was on a ship bound for England. His room was tiny and dark. The fourth night out he awoke, gasping for air. The room seemed to be closing in on him. He felt trapped. His distress was so great that he began to panic. If ever he needed God to have pity on him and come to his aid, it was now. He yearned for the light of God's face to shine down on him and to fill his heart with calm. David said later that this terrifying experience gave him new insight into Psalm 4.

When I call, answer me, O my just God,
you who relieve me when I am in distress;
Have pity on me, and hear my prayer!

Know that the LORD does wonders
for his faithful one;
the LORD will hear me when I call upon him.

O LORD, let the light of your countenance
shine upon us!
You put gladness into my heart.

As soon as I lie down, I fall peacefully asleep,
for you alone, O LORD,
bring security to my dwelling.   (2, 4, 7–8, 9)

Jesus undoubtedly experienced a feeling like this when he was imprisoned the night before his crucifixion. Along with Psalm 3, he may have also prayed this psalm.

Recall a time when things seemed to close in on you and cause you to panic. Speak to Jesus about how he kept calm at such moments.

Day five   Psalm **5**

Lead me in your justice, Lord.

In his novel *East of Eden*, John Steinbeck says, "I believe there is one story in the world. . . . Humans are caught . . . in a net of good and evil. . . . There is no other story. A man, after he has brushed off the dust and chips of life, will have left only the hard, clean question: Was it good or was it evil? Have I done well—or ill?" The Hebrew psalmist would have applauded Steinbeck's insight.

At dawn I bring my plea
expectantly before you.
For you, O God, delight not in wickedness;
no evil man remains with you;
the arrogant may not stand in your sight.

You hate all evildoers;
you destroy all who speak falsehood;
The bloodthirsty and the deceitful
the LORD abhors.

But I, because of your abundant kindness,
will enter your house;
I will worship at your holy temple
in fear of you, O LORD.   (4–9)

Jesus taught a final judgment, saying, "When the Son of Man comes in his glory . . . all the nations will be assembled before him. And he will separate them one from another, as a shepherd separates the sheep from the goats." *Matthew 25:31–32*

Evaluate your life up to this point in time. Speak to Jesus about any changes you might make.

Day six   Psalm 6

Rescue me because of your kindness.

One of George Washington's first tasks as commander-in-chief of the American troops was to expel Captain John Callender from the army for cowardice at Bunker Hill. Later, Callender reenlisted as a private and fought with such bravery in the Battle of Long Island that Washington restored him to his rank of captain. The psalmist prays that God will treat him with similar kindness and compassion.

O Lord, reprove me not in your anger,
nor chastise me in your wrath.
Have pity on me, O Lord,
for my body is in terror.

Return, O Lord, save my life;
rescue me because of your kindness.
I drench my couch with my tears.
My eyes are dimmed with sorrow.

Depart from me, all evildoers,
for the Lord has heard the sound of my weeping;
The Lord has heard my plea;
the Lord has accepted my prayer.   (2-3, 5, 7-8, 9-10)

The heart of Jesus was filled with compassion for sinners. No doubt he pondered seven penitential psalms long and lovingly.   (Psalms 6, 32, 38, 51, 102, 130, 143)

Imagine Jesus telling the parable of the lost sheep. Study his face and eyes as he concludes it, saying, "There will be more joy in heaven over one sinner who repents than over ninety-nine righteous people who have no need of repentance."   *Luke 15:7*   Speak to Jesus about his forgiveness of your sins.

Day *seven*   Psalm 7

Lord, my God, I take shelter in you.

In 1987 a newspaper headline read, "Blacks Gather to Mourn Dead in South Africa." The article went on to say, "Blacks gathered by the tens of thousands Friday to mourn their dead. . . . Witnesses said police broke up one ceremony with rubber whips and birdshot." The suffering of these innocent blacks helps us better understand the feelings expressed in Psalm 7.

> *O Lord, my God, in you I take refuge;*
> *save me from all my pursuers and rescue me,*
> *Lest I become like the lion's prey,*
> *to be torn to pieces, with no one to rescue me.*
>
> *Do me justice, O Lord, because I am just,*
> *and because of the innocence that is mine.*
> *Let the malice of the wicked come to an end,*
> *but sustain the just,*
> *O searcher of heart and soul, O just God.*
>
> *A shield before me is God,*
> *who saves the upright of heart;*
> *A just judge is God,*
> *a God who punishes day by day.*   (2–3, 9–12)

Jesus' heart went out to suffering people. The Gospel records that on numerous occasions "his heart was moved with pity for them, for they were like sheep without a shepherd." *Mark 6:34*

Speak to Jesus about the mystery of why so many innocent people suffer at the hands of evil people. Ask him what you can do in the face of this mystery.

O Lord, our God, how wonderful your name in all the earth!

On Sunday, July 20, 1969, the first manned spacecraft from Earth landed on the moon. Before returning to Earth again, astronauts Armstrong and Aldrin placed on the moon a capsule containing a copy of Psalm 8.

When I behold your heavens,
the work of your fingers,
the moon and the stars which you set in place—
What is man that you should be mindful of him,
or the son of man that you should care for him?

You have made him little less than the angels,
and crowned him with glory and honor.
You have given him rule over the works
of your hands,
putting all things under his feet:

All sheep and oxen,
yes, and the beasts of the field,
The birds of the air, the fishes of the sea,
and whatever swims the paths of the seas.   (4-9)

Jesus often prayed outdoors. Thus, before choosing his twelve apostles, he climbed a high hill and "spent the night in prayer." *Luke 6:12*   Surely Jesus prayed this psalm that memorable night.

It is night. Like Jesus, you are outdoors, and the moon is bright enough for you to read this psalm. Read it meditatively, pausing after each verse for a few minutes of silent communion with God.

The Lord will judge the world with justice.

The famous sportswriter Grantland Rice wrote a poem that ends with these lines: "For when the One Great Scorer comes / To write against your name, / He marks—not that you won or lost— / But how you played the game." God's judgment was also a thought that the Hebrew psalmist pondered and reflected on regularly.

I will give thanks to you, O LORD,
  with all my heart;
    I will declare all your wondrous deeds.
I will be glad and exult in you;
  I will sing praise to your name, Most High.

You rebuked the nations and destroyed the wicked;
  their name you blotted out forever and ever.
The nations are sunk in the pit they have made;
  in the snare they set, their foot is caught.

But the LORD sits enthroned forever;
  he has set up his throne for judgment.
He judges the world with justice;
  he governs the peoples with equity.   (2–3, 6, 16, 8–9)

Paul writes: "We must all appear before the judgment seat of Christ, so that each one may receive recompense, according to what he did in the body, whether good or evil." *2 Corinthians 5:10*

Some people fear the idea of a final judgment. What do you fear most about it? Speak to Jesus about your fears, and ask him to calm them.

Do not forget the poor, O Lord!

As Dietrich Bonhoeffer awaited death in a Nazi prison, he saw no evidence of God. Yet the faith expressed in this psalm sustained him.

Why, O Lord, do you stand aloof?
Why hide in times of distress?
    Proudly the wicked harass the afflicted,
    who are caught in the devices
       the wicked have contrived.

For the wicked man glories in his greed,
    and the covetous blasphemes,
       sets the Lord at nought.
The wicked man boasts, "He will not avenge it";
    "There is no God," sums up his thoughts.

His mouth is full of cursing, guile and deceit;
    under his tongue are mischief and iniquity.
He lurks in ambush near the villages;
    in hiding he murders the innocent;
    his eyes spy upon the unfortunate.

You do see, for you behold misery and sorrow,
    taking them in your hands.
On you the unfortunate man depends;
    of the fatherless you are the helper.   (1–4, 7–8, 14)

Jesus, too, knew soul-wrenching moments, similar to those expressed in this psalm.

Recall a soul-wrenching moment in your life. Speak to God about the purpose of such moments.

In the Lord 1 take refuge.

A recurring theme in the psalms is the battle in this world between good and evil. Two options are open when good people meet evil face-to-face. They can stand their ground and—with God's help—do something about it, or they can "flee to the mountain." In this psalm, the good man chooses to stand his ground and do something about it, even though his friend counsels otherwise.

> *In the LORD I take refuge;*
>   *how can you say to me,*
>   *"Flee to the mountain like a bird!*
> *For, see, the wicked*
>   *shoot in the dark at the upright."*
>
> *The LORD is in his holy temple;*
>   *the LORD's throne is in heaven.*
> *His eyes behold,*
>   *his searching glance is on mankind.*
>
> *The LORD searches the just and the wicked;*
>   *the lover of violence he hates.*
> *For the LORD is just, he loves just deeds;*
>   *the upright shall see his face.*   (1–2, 4–5, 7)

In his parable of the good Samaritan, Jesus dramatizes the two options that are open when good people come face-to-face with evil or its effects. The Samaritan stands his ground; the priest and the Levite flee.   (Luke 10:30–37)

How do you react when you come face-to-face with evil or its effects? Speak to Jesus about this.

Day five

Psalm 12

You will protect us, Lord.

In 1799 prophets of doom were predicting that the end of the century would also be the end of the world. France had just endured a bloody revolution; Europe was in chaos; and the situation in Rome was so bad that the cardinals had to meet in Venice to elect a new pope. Many believed this would be their last pope. Psalm 12 took on special meaning.

Help, O Lord! for no one now is dutiful;
faithfulness has vanished from among men.
Everyone speaks falsehood to his neighbor;
with smooth lips they speak, and double heart.

May the Lord destroy all smooth lips,
every boastful tongue,
Those who say, "We are heroes with our tongues;
our lips are our own; who is lord over us?"

The promises of the Lord are sure,
like tried silver, freed from dross,
sevenfold refined.
You, O Lord, will keep us
and preserve us always from this generation.

(2–5, 7–8)

Times were also bad in Jesus' day. Speaking out against evil leaders, Jesus said, "Woe to you, scribes and Pharisees, you hypocrites. You are like whitewashed tombs, which appear beautiful on the outside, but inside are full of . . . filth." *Matthew 23:27*

Does evil and evil leadership in our world depress you? Speak to Jesus about how he maintained faith, hope, and love in the midst of an evil world.

All my hope, O Lord,
is in your loving kindness.

Father Walter Ciszek, an American Jesuit, spent twenty-three years in Russia, most of the time in prison or slave labor camps in Siberia. "One day," he says, "the blackness closed in around me completely.... I had crossed over into a pit of blackness I had never known before." Psalm 13 describes his thoughts.

How long, O Lord? Will you utterly forget me?
　How long will you hide your face from me?
　　How long shall I harbor sorrow in my soul,
　grief in my heart day after day?
How long will my enemy triumph over me?
　Look, answer me, O Lord, my God!

Give light to my eyes that I may not sleep in death
　lest my enemy say, "I have overcome him";
Lest my foes rejoice at my downfall
　though I trusted in your kindness.

Let my heart rejoice in your salvation;
　let me sing of the Lord,
　　"He has been good to me."　(2–6)

Jesus, too, knew moments of darkness. On the cross he cried out, "My God, my God, why have you forsaken me?" *Mark 15:34*

How sensitive are you to people suffering from abandonment or rejection, like a senior citizen in a nursing home? An abandoned spouse? Speak to Jesus about someone you know who needs comfort and love at this moment.

Day *seven*   Psalm **14**

God will rescue his people.

The Empire Strikes Back is a modern morality play. The galaxy has fallen under the control of the evil Darth Vader. Despair is everywhere. No one gives young Luke Skywalker much of a chance as he goes forth to do battle with the evil tyrant. But Luke knows what the rest of the galaxy doesn't know: The Force is with him. The world of evil into which Luke stepped was much like the world described in Psalm 14.

> *he Lord looks down from heaven*
> *upon the children of men,*
> *to see if there be one who is wise*
> *and seeks God.*
>
> *All alike have gone astray;*
> *they have become perverse;*
> *there is not one who does good, not even one.*
>
> *When the Lord restores the well-being*
> *of his people,*
> *then shall Jacob exult and Israel be glad.*   (2–3, 7)

Jesus stepped into a world just like the one portrayed in *The Empire Strikes Back*. He too wasn't given much of a chance by many. But he too knew what they didn't know: The Spirit was with him.

How hopeful are you that you can battle the evil of the world, as did Luke in his science-fiction world and Jesus in his real world? Speak to Jesus about the Spirit that he has given to you.

For reflection or discussion

INTRODUCTION Why is a responsorial psalm so-called? Why does it usually follow an Old Testament reading? What two purposes did the Book of Psalms serve in Israel? Explain: "To sing is to pray twice." What are three settings in which Israel prayed or sang the psalms?

WEEK 1
1   Bearing fruit
How do you understand Jesus' words, "A tree is known by its fruit"?

Recall a recent fruit in your life: something you did to advance God's work.

What are some things you could do to advance God's work? What keeps you from doing them?

2   Forgiving
Why would you agree/disagree that it is harder to forgive a friend than it is to forgive an enemy?

Recall a person (and what he or she did) that you still have not *fully* forgiven.

What are some things you might do to help you forgive that person? What keeps you from doing them?

WEEK 2
1   Evil
Explain: "The only thing necessary for evil to triumph is for good people to do nothing."   *Edmund Burke*

Recall a time when you did, or failed to do, something about evil.

What are some current evils, and what might you do about them? What keeps you from doing these things?

2   Suffering
Explain: "Jesus did not come to do away with suffering or remove it. He came to fill it with his presence."   *Paul Claudel*

Recall a time when you felt God's presence in mental or physical suffering.

Think of some suffering people. What might you do to help them experience God's presence in their suffering? Why might these things give them a sense of God's presence?

Who Wrote the Psalms?

2 *When the LORD saved David . . .
David sang this song to the LORD.*
2 Samuel 22:1 (TEV)

Imagine you are strolling alone in a woods on a spring day. You let your eyes follow the trunk of a tree as it stretches toward the sky and the sun. As you marvel at the beauty of it all, you have no idea who planted the tree. But it really doesn't matter. It's there! And that's all that counts.

The Book of Psalms is like that. When you page through it, you are not always sure who wrote the psalm you are looking at. But it really doesn't matter. It's there! And that's all that counts.

Sometimes David's name appears in the notes that introduce the psalms. But these notes were added by later editors and may simply mean that a psalm was dedicated to David or was approved by him. It is not always too clear what the note means.

How many psalms did David write? We don't know. We do know, however, that many psalms date from David's time: 1000 B.C. We also know that tradition gives David credit for authoring many of the psalms. Finally, we know that David was a gifted poet and a skilled musician. (1 Samuel 16:17–23, 1 Chronicles 25:1–8)   But that is about all we know for sure about his role in writing the psalms.

19

Some of the psalms to which David's name is linked are the following. After each psalm, reference is given to an event in David's life to which the psalm could refer.

Psalm 3	Absalom's rebellion (2 Samuel 15:13ff.)
Psalm 18	David's victory song (2 Samuel 22)
Psalm 34	David's faked madness (1 Samuel 21)
Psalm 51	David's sin (2 Samuel 11–12)
Psalm 52	Doeg's betrayal of the priests (1 Samuel 22)
Psalm 54	The Ziphite informers (1 Samuel 23:19ff.)
Psalm 57	David in the cave (1 Samuel 22:1–2)
Psalm 59	David's escape (1 Samuel 19:11ff.)
Psalm 60	Victory over Edomites (2 Samuel 8:13)
Psalm 63	David in the desert (1 Samuel 24:1–2)
Psalm 142	David in the cave (1 Samuel 24:3ff.)

He who does justice
will live in the presence of the Lord.

Picture pilgrims who have come from distant towns to worship in Jerusalem. Priests stop them at the entrance to the Temple and lead them in singing or chanting the following "ten commandments." Only then may they enter the "Lord's tent" and worship.

O Lord, who shall sojourn in your tent?
Who shall dwell on your holy mountain?

He who walks blamelessly and does justice;
who thinks the truth in his heart
and slanders not with his tongue;

Who harms not his fellow man,
nor takes up a reproach against his neighbor;
By whom the reprobate is despised,
while he honors those who fear the Lord;

Who, though it be to his loss,
changes not his pledged word;
who lends not his money at usury
and accepts no bribe against the innocent.

He who does these things
shall never be disturbed.   (1–5)

Jesus sang this psalm before entering the Temple with his parents at the age of twelve.

Imagine yourself standing next to the twelve-year-old Jesus as he sang this psalm outside his Father's house. Speak to him about his feelings. About your feelings.

21   WEEK 3

Lord, you will show us the path of life.

It is Pentecost! You are in the crowd, listening to Peter explain what has just happened. Listen to Peter recite the last half of this psalm from memory as he applies it to Jesus' resurrection. (Acts 2:25–28)

*K*eep me, O God, for in you I take refuge;
   I say to the Lord, "My Lord are you."
   O Lord, my allotted portion and my cup,
you it is who hold fast my lot.

I bless the Lord who counsels me;
   even in the night my heart exhorts me.
I set the Lord ever before me;
   with him at my right hand I shall not be disturbed.

Therefore my heart is glad and my soul rejoices,
   my body, too, abides in confidence;
Because you will not abandon my soul
    to the nether world,
   nor will you suffer your faithful one
    to undergo corruption.

You will show me the path to life,
   fullness of joys in your presence,
   the delights at your right hand forever. (1–2, 5, 7–11)

Paul also cited this same psalm when talking to the Jews about Jesus' resurrection. (Acts 13:35)

Recite the last half of this psalm as Peter must have recited it to the crowd. Try to imagine what Peter felt. Speak to Jesus about your feelings.

Lord, when your glory appears, my joy will be full.

The Book of Job is about a good man. He has spent his whole life doing good. Then one day a series of tragedies befalls him. Job can't understand why all this is happening to him, because he has kept God's law as perfectly as any person could. We can imagine Job, with tears in his eyes, looking up to the heavens and praying this psalm from his heart.

Hear, O LORD, a just suit;
attend to my outcry;
hearken to my prayer from lips without deceit.

I call upon you, for you will answer me, O God;
incline your ear to me; hear my word.
Show your wondrous kindness,
O savior of those who flee from their foes.

Hide me in the shadow of your wings.
But I in justice shall behold your face;
on waking, I shall be content in your presence.

(1, 6–7, 8, 15)

The person in this psalm is like the rich young man in the Gospel who had kept all the commandments from his youth. "Jesus, looking at him, loved him." *Mark 10:21*   Without doubt, God loved the person in this psalm, also.

The famous Scottish preacher Alexander Whyte had the final line of this psalm inscribed on his tombstone. Picture Jesus looking at you and loving you as you awake in his presence on the last day. Speak to Jesus about that moment.

Day four   Psalm 18

In my distress I called upon the Lord, and he heard my voice.

The Book of Samuel says, "David sang the words of this song to the Lord when the Lord had rescued him from the grasp of all his enemies and from the hand of Saul." *2 Samuel 22:1*

I love you, O Lord, my strength,
O Lord, my rock, my fortress, my deliverer.

My God, my rock of refuge,
my shield, the horn of my salvation, my stronghold!
Praised be the Lord, I exclaim,
and I am safe from my enemies.

The breakers of death surged round about me,
the destroying floods overwhelmed me;
The cords of the nether world enmeshed me,
the snares of death overtook me.

In my distress I called upon the Lord
and cried out to my God;
From his temple he heard my voice,
and my cry to him reached his ears. (2-7)

Jesus may also have prayed this psalm at Nazareth after escaping the angry mob who planned to "hurl him down headlong" over a cliff. *Luke 4:29*

Recall a close encounter with death that you had. Relive the event. Speak to Jesus about whether you may have been saved from death for some special purpose.

The heavens proclaim the glory of God.

Letters from the Desert by Carlo Carretto is a journal of a person who went into the desert to learn to pray. Carlo writes: "The first nights spent here made me send off for books on astronomy. . . . For months afterwards I spent my free time learning a little of what was passing over my head up there in the universe. . . . Kneeling on the sand I sank my eyes for hours and hours into those wonders, writing down my discoveries in an exercise book like a child. . . . How dear they were to me, those stars; how close to them the desert had brought me." What Carlo saw kneeling in the sand, the psalmist also saw. Filled with awe, he wrote:

> *The heavens declare the glory of God,*
> *and the firmament proclaims his handiwork.*
> *Day pours out the word to day,*
> *and night to night imparts knowledge;*
>
> *Not a word nor a discourse*
> *whose voice is not heard;*
> *Through all the earth their voice resounds,*
> *and to the ends of the world, their message.* (2–5)

Jesus also spent whole nights under the stars. On one of those nights he may have recited this psalm.

Recall a time when you gazed up at the stars in wonder. Speak to God about the "message" the stars speak to the "ends of the world."

Day six   Psalm 20

Lord, answer us when we call upon you.

Picture yourself in Jerusalem the night before a great battle. Outside the city walls an enemy army is encamped. In the morning the king and his soldiers must defend the city. Now the king sits on a throne in the temple area. Surrounding him are his troops and his subjects, holding blazing torches. The high priest stands, turns to the king, and says in a loud voice that echoes off the walls of the Temple:

> *he Lord answer you in time of distress;*
> *the name of the God of Jacob defend you!*
> *May he grant you what is in your heart*
> *and fulfill your every plan.*

> *Now I know that the Lord has given victory*
> *to his anointed,*
> *that he has answered him from his holy heaven*
> *with the strength of his victorious right hand.*

> *Some are strong in chariots; some, in horses;*
> *but we are strong in the name of the Lord.*
> *O Lord, grant victory to the king,*
> *and answer us when we call upon you.*   (2, 5, 7–8, 10)

This psalm has been used to bless missionaries as they set off to preach the Gospel of Jesus, often in hostile and life-threatening situations.

How deep is your faith and trust that God is with you, strengthening and supporting you in time of need? Speak to Jesus about how you can deepen your faith and trust in God and his concern for you.

Lord, your strength gives joy to the king.

A fable describes a rooster who arrogantly believed the sun rose because he crowed. Some kings have possessed a similar arrogance. Israel's kings—at least the good ones—never had that problem. They knew that it was God who crowned them, gave them victory over evil enemies, strengthened them, and blessed them with their heart's desire. For this they were filled with profound joy and gratitude. They prayed humbly:

> *O* LORD, *in your strength the king is glad;*
> *in your victory how greatly he rejoices!*
> *You have granted him his heart's desire;*
> *you refused not the wish of his lips.*
>
> *For you welcomed him with goodly blessings,*
> *you placed on his head a crown of pure gold.*
> *He asked life of you: you gave him*
> *length of days forever and ever.*
>
> *Great is his glory in your victory;*
> *majesty and splendor you conferred upon him.*
> *For you made him a blessing forever;*
> *you gladdened him with the joy of your presence.*
>
> (2–7)

The model for all persons in authority was Jesus, the King of Kings, who said, "The Son of Man did not come to be served but to serve." *Mark 10:45*

What is your attitude toward those under your authority? Toward your talents? Toward the blessings God has showered upon you? Speak to Jesus about these things.

Day one   Psalm 22

My God, my God,
why have you abandoned me?

Picture boys and girls chained together in a Gaza slave market. Taken from their Jewish village in a raid, they stand naked, waiting to be sold. Their emotions vacillate from despair to hope that God will rescue them. A scene like this inspired this psalm.

All who see me scoff at me;
they mock me with parted lips,
they wag their heads:
"He relied on the LORD; let him deliver him,
let him rescue him, if he loves him."

Indeed, many dogs surround me,
a pack of evildoers closes in upon me;
They have pierced my hands and my feet;
I can count all my bones.

They divide my garments among them,
and for my vesture they cast lots.
But you, O LORD, be not far from me;
O my help, hasten to aid me.

I will proclaim your name to my brethren;
in the midst of the assembly I will praise you:
"You who fear the LORD, praise him;
all you descendants of Jacob, give glory to him."
(8–9, 17–18, 19–20, 23–24)

Jesus prayed this psalm on the cross when his enemies surrounded and mocked him, pierced his hands and feet, and cast lots for his clothes.   (Mark 15:24–34)

How do you pray in time of suffering? Do you unite your suffering with that of Jesus? Recite this psalm as Jesus must have spoken it on the cross.

The Lord is my shepherd, there is nothing I shall want.

American POWs in Vietnam knew moments of fear and darkness. Postwar interviews of prisoners reveal that the most popular prayer in these moments was Psalm 23.

The LORD is my shepherd; I shall not want.
In verdant pastures he gives me repose;
Beside restful waters he leads me;
he refreshes my soul.

He guides me in the right paths
for his name's sake.
Even though I walk in the dark valley
I fear no evil; for you are at my side
With your rod and your staff
that give me courage.

You spread the table before me
in the sight of my foes;
You anoint my head with oil;
my cup overflows.

Only goodness and kindness follow me
all the days of my life;
And I shall dwell in the house of the LORD
for years to come. (1–6)

Speaking through the prophet, God said of his people, "I will give them a king like my servant David to be their one shepherd." *Ezekiel 34:23 (TEV)*

Imagine the thoughts that leaped into people's minds when Jesus said, "I am the good shepherd." *John 10:11* Speak to Jesus about your own thoughts.

Day three   Psalm 24

Who is the king of glory? It is the Lord!

David was crowned Israel's king in 1000 B.C. After making Jerusalem his political capital, he made it his religious capital as well. A sanctuary was built, and when all was ready, a great procession escorted the ark of the covenant (sign of God's presence) to the city. When the procession reached the city gates, all Jerusalem exploded in song. (2 Samuel 6:1–15)

Lift up, O gates, your lintels;
reach up, you ancient portals,
that the king of glory may come in!

Who is this king of glory?
The LORD, strong and mighty,
the LORD, mighty in battle.

Lift up, O gates, your lintels;
reach up, you ancient portals,
that the king of glory may come in!

Who is this king of glory?
The LORD of hosts; he is the king of glory. (7–10)

On Palm Sunday Jesus rode a donkey to Jerusalem. As he approached the city, the words of Psalm 24 must have echoed in the minds of many as they paved the road with palm branches and broke into song. The Lord, the "king of glory," was about to enter the "ancient portals" of the city.

How do you welcome the king of glory into your own heart in the celebration of the Eucharist? Speak to Jesus about how you could do this even better.

Teach me your ways, O Lord.

While seeking God's guidance, John Cardinal Newman wrote these lines of a now-famous hymn: "Lead, kindly Light, amid the encircling gloom, / Lead Thou me on! / The night is dark, and I am far from home, / Lead Thou me on; / Keep Thou my feet; I do not ask to see / The distant scene—one step enough for me." Newman's lines recall a similar prayer for guidance, penned by the psalmist.

our ways, O Lord, make known to me;
teach me your paths.
Guide me in your truth and teach me,
for you are God my savior.

Remember that your compassion, O Lord,
and your kindness are from of old.
In your kindness remember me,
because of your goodness, O Lord.

Good and upright is the Lord;
thus he shows sinners the way.
He guides the humble to justice,
he teaches the humble his way.   (4–5, 6, 7–9)

When Thomas asked Jesus for guidance, Jesus said to him, "I am the way."   *John 14:6*

In what sense does Jesus hold the answer in your own search for guidance in times of doubt or decision–making? Speak to Jesus about this.

Psalm 26

O Lord, your kindness is before my eyes.

Picture an Israelite who has been accused of a serious crime. Insisting upon his innocence, he stands before the temple altar and swears to God that he is not guilty. Psalm 26 puts us in touch with this dramatic ritual, described in 1 Kings 8:31–32.

> *S*earch me, O LORD, and try me;
>   *test my soul and my heart.*
>   *For your kindness is before my eyes,*
> *and I walk in your truth.*
>
> *I wash my hands in innocence,*
>   *and I go around your altar, O LORD,*
> *Giving voice to my thanks,*
>   *and recounting all your wondrous deeds.*
> *O LORD, I love the house in which you dwell,*
>   *the tenting-place of your glory.*
>
> *Gather not my soul with those of sinners,*
>   *nor with men of blood my life.*
> *On their hands are crimes,*
>   *and their right hands are full of bribes.*
>
> *But I walk in integrity;*
>   *redeem me, and have pity on me.*
> *My foot stands on level ground;*
>   *in the assemblies I will bless the LORD.*   (2–3, 6–12)

Paul writes, "In every way you have shown yourselves to be innocent in the matter."   *2 Corinthians 7:11*

Speak to Jesus about a time when you were falsely accused or judged. Forgive those involved.

The Lord is my light and my salvation.

Charles Colson, aide to President Nixon, went to prison as a result of Watergate. Describing early hours of the scandal, he writes in *Born Again:* "Deep down I knew I would be among those indicted. . . . I kept smiling, hoping and reciting the Twenty-seventh Psalm over and over."

he Lord is my light and my salvation;
*   whom should I fear?*
*   The Lord is my life's refuge;*
of whom should I be afraid?

Hear, O Lord, the sound of my call;
*   have pity on me, and answer me.*
Of you my heart speaks; you my glance seeks;
*   your presence, O Lord, I seek.*

Hide not your face from me;
*   do not in anger repel your servant.*
You are my helper: cast me not off.

I believe that I shall see the bounty of the Lord
*   in the land of the living.*
Wait for the Lord with courage;
*   be stouthearted, and wait for the Lord.*   (1, 7-9, 13-14)

"If God is for us, who can be against us? . . . There is nothing in all creation that will ever be able to separate us from the love of God which is ours through Christ Jesus."   *Romans 8:31, 39 (TEV)*

Speak to Jesus about what keeps you from trusting and giving yourself over to him more fully.

Blest be the Lord
for he has heard my prayer.

Jews regarded Jerusalem as the holiest city in the world.
And the holiest building in the city was the Temple. And
the holiest room in the Temple was the holy shrine, where
the ark of the covenant was housed. Jews often faced toward the holy shrine and prayed with uplifted hands. The
psalmist prays this way in this psalm. The tone of his prayer
is one of humble, childlike trust.

Hear the sound of my pleading,
when I cry to you,
lifting up my hands toward your holy shrine.

The LORD is my strength and my shield.
In him my heart trusts, and I find help;
then my heart exults, and with my song
I give him thanks.

The LORD is the strength of his people,
the saving refuge of his anointed.
Save your people, and bless your inheritance;
feed them, and carry them forever!   (2, 7–9)

Jesus told a parable about two men praying in the
Temple. One exalted himself; the other humbled himself.
Jesus condemned the former and praised the latter, saying,
"Everyone who exalts himself will be humbled, and the one
who humbles himself will be exalted."   Luke 18:14

How humble is your prayer? How trustful? Speak to
Jesus about what you could do to improve the quality of
your prayer.

For reflection or discussion

INTRODUCTION   In some Bibles the psalms are introduced by brief notes. Who made these notes? What evidence suggests David's role in writing the psalms? Compare Psalm 18 with 2 Samuel 22. How might you explain the similarities and differences?

WEEK 3
1   Death
Explain: "In the night of death, hope sees a star, and listening love hears the rustle of a wing."   *Anonymous*

Recall your closest encounter with death and the things that went through your mind then.

Think of some friends who are approaching death. What might you do for them? Which of these things would be most appreciated by them? Why not do it?

2   Leadership
Explain: "You can't lead anyone else further than you have gone yourself."   *Gene Mauch*

Recall a time when you took the lead in doing something that needed doing in your community.

What are some areas that need leadership that you could provide? What keeps you from providing it?

WEEK 4
1   Decision-making
Explain: "It's the age-old struggle—the roar of the crowd on one side and the voice of your conscience on the other."   *General Douglas MacArthur*

Recall a difficult decision you made that involved both of these sides.

What is one decision you are putting off? What keeps you from acting more decisively?

2   Humility
Explain: "Humility is not thinking little of self; it's not thinking of self at all."   *Anonymous*

Recall a humiliating or embarrassing occasion in your life and how you reacted to it.

Who is one of the humblest persons you know? How do you account for that person's humility, and what keeps you from emulating him or her?

35

Themes of the Psalms

3 *God sent his Singers upon earth . . .*
That they might touch the hearts of men,
And bring them back to heaven again.

Henry Wadsworth Longfellow

The movie *The Sound of Music* contains a show-stopping song called "Maria." One line from the song asks, "How do you hold a moonbeam in your hand?" That line celebrates the fact that Maria is so special that she is in a class by herself.

Many of the psalms are like Maria. They too are in a class by themselves. Trying to classify them is like trying to hold a moonbeam in your hand. Nevertheless, one attempt to classify the psalms divides them into five groups: praise, wisdom, royal, thanksgiving, and lament.

Praise psalms concern God's glory and often begin with the words "Praise the Lord."

> *Praise the LORD in his sanctuary.*
> *Praise him with timbrel and dance,*
> *praise him with strings and pipe.*   Psalm 150:1, 4

Wisdom psalms concern human conduct and often begin with the words "Happy is he."

Happy is he who has regard
for the lowly and the poor;
in the day of misfortune
the LORD will deliver him.   Psalm 41:2

Royal psalms concern the king. Beginning with God's promise to David, the king became more than a political figure. He became a religious symbol as well. Each new king brought the world closer to the "King of Kings," the promised Messiah.

O God, with your judgment endow the king.
All kings shall pay him homage,
all nations shall serve him.   Psalm 72:1, 11

Thanksgiving psalms express gratitude to God for some benefit or blessing.

You changed my mourning into dancing;
you took off my sackcloth
and clothed me with gladness.
O LORD, my God, forever will I give you thanks.
Psalm 30:12, 13

Finally, lament psalms are "songs of woe" in which the psalmist pours out his heart to God about some situation. They often deal with defeat at the hands of an enemy or injury at the hands of a wicked man.

I am sleepless, and I moan;
I am like a sparrow alone on the housetop.
All the day my enemies revile me.   Psalm 102:8–9

Whether or not the psalms can be fitted into neat categories is unimportant. What is important is whether or not they speak to the heart.

Day one

Psalm 29

The Lord will bless his people with peace.

Called the "Song of the Seven Thunders," this psalm mentions the "voice of the LORD" seven times. Perhaps this is a reference to the seven days of creation, when the same voice of God called into being the world and everything in it.

Give to the LORD, you sons of God,
give to the LORD glory and praise,
Give to the LORD the glory due his name;
adore the LORD in holy attire.

The voice of the LORD is over the waters,
the God of glory thunders,
the LORD, over vast waters.
The voice of the LORD is mighty;
the voice of the LORD is majestic.

The voice of the LORD breaks the cedars.
The voice of the LORD strikes fiery flames;
the voice of the LORD shakes the desert.
The voice of the LORD twists the oaks,
and in his temple all say, "Glory!"

The LORD is enthroned above the flood;
the LORD is enthroned as king forever. (1–5, 7–8, 9–10)

Early Christians connected this psalm with Jesus' baptism. When the sky opened, "a voice came from heaven," saying, "You are my beloved Son." *Luke 3:22*

When and where do you hear the Lord's voice most clearly today? Speak to the Lord about this.

I will praise you, Lord, for you have rescued me.

The way a band plays off a comic after he delivers his last line can determine how much applause he gets. Bands playing in London subways bolstered people's morale during World War II air raids. Music touches people deeply. Small wonder the psalmist turns to images of song and dance after being rescued from death.

*I will extol you, O Lord, for you drew me clear
and did not let my enemies rejoice over me.
O Lord, you brought me up
from the nether world;
you preserved me from among those
going down into the pit.*

*Sing praise to the Lord, you his faithful ones,
and give thanks to his holy name.
For his anger lasts but a moment;
a lifetime, his good will.
At nightfall, weeping enters in,
but with the dawn, rejoicing.*

*Hear, O Lord, and have pity on me;
O Lord, be my helper.
You changed my mourning into dancing;
O Lord, my God, forever will I give you thanks.*
(2, 4–6, 11–12, 13)

Early Christians applied this psalm to Jesus and his resurrection from the dead.

Recall a time when God changed your "mourning into dancing." Speak to Jesus about it.

Day three   Psalm 31

Into your hands, O Lord,
I entrust my spirit.

In February 1953, two escaped soldiers, Tiira and Ericsson, were adrift in the Indian Ocean on a four-foot raft. They had no food and only rain to drink. On the seventeenth day Ericsson died. For the next two weeks Tiira drifted alone, battling thirst, starvation, and possible capture. On the thirty-first day, the day before his rescue, Tiira sensed death was near and placed himself totally in God's hands. Psalm 31 expresses his feelings.

Be my rock of refuge,
a stronghold to give me safety.
You are my rock and my fortress;
for your name's sake you will lead and guide me.

Into your hands I commend my spirit;
you will redeem me, O LORD, O faithful God.
My trust is in the LORD.
I will rejoice and be glad of your kindness.

Let your face shine upon your servant;
save me in your kindness.
You hide those who fear you
in the shelter of your presence
from the plottings of men.   (3–4, 6, 7–8, 17, 21)

On the cross, Jesus placed himself in his Father's hands, using the words of Psalm 31.   (Luke 23:46)

Recall a time when you placed yourself completely in God's hands. Speak to Jesus about any fear you have in turning your future over to the Father for whatever he may wish to do with it.

Lord, forgive the wrong 1 have done.

Paul Buchanan had avoided the sacrament of Reconciliation for two years. Finally he overcame his fear and went. Afterward he took a drive and came upon an old chapel. He stopped and went in. "Everything, even the burning candles," he wrote later, "had an air of simple beauty. . . . Then, on the left side of the sanctuary at the foot of the altar, I noticed a wooden lectern standing by itself. On it was a Bible. . . . I walked forward and began to read. It was open to Psalm 32."

> *appy is he whose fault is taken away,*
> *whose sin is covered.*
> *Happy the man to whom the LORD*
> *imputes not guilt,*
> *in whose spirit there is no guile.*
>
> *Then I acknowledged my sin to you,*
> *my guilt I covered not.*
> *I said, "I confess my faults to the LORD,"*
> *and you took away the guilt of my sin.*
>
> *Be glad in the LORD and rejoice, you just;*
> *exult, all you upright of heart.*   (1–2, 5, 11)

Jesus said, "There will be more joy in heaven over one sinner who repents than over ninety-nine righteous people who have no need of repentance."   *Luke 15:7*

What keeps you from seeking God's forgiveness more frequently? Speak to Jesus, the Good Shepherd, about it.

*Cry out with joy in the Lord,
you holy ones; sing a new song to him.*

Someone asked an old desert nomad how he could be so sure there was a God. The nomad replied, "The same way I can be so sure that a man or an animal has just crossed the desert sand. I see God's footprints everywhere I look."

*Give thanks to the LORD on the harp;
with the ten-stringed lyre chant his praises.
Sing to him a new song;
pluck the strings skillfully, with shouts of gladness.*

*The plan of the LORD stands forever;
the design of his heart, through all generations.
Happy the nation whose God is the LORD,
the people he has chosen for his own inheritance.*

*Our soul waits for the LORD,
who is our help and our shield,
For in him our hearts rejoice;
in his holy name we trust.* (2–3, 11–12, 20–21)

Each new experience of God calls for a "new song" of praise. Thus, in John's vision of heaven, the elders "fell down before [Jesus] the Lamb. Each of the elders held a harp" and together "they sang a new hymn." *Revelation 5:8–9*

Recall a time when you had an experience of God or God's love that made you want to sing for joy. Relive it in your memory. Speak to God about the footprints that he has left behind in his creation.

Day six  Psalm 34

Taste and see the goodness of the Lord.

A Bible that Abraham Lincoln used while in the White House falls open easily to Psalm 34. A smudge in the margin shows where the president's thumb rested as he meditated on it often.

I will bless the LORD at all times;
his praise shall be ever in my mouth.
Let my soul glory in the LORD;
the lowly will hear me and be glad.

Glorify the LORD with me,
let us together extol his name.
I sought the LORD, and he answered me
and delivered me from all my fears.

Look to him that you may be radiant with joy,
and your faces may not blush with shame.
When the afflicted man called out, the LORD heard,
and from all his distress he saved him.   (2–7)

On one occasion David escaped capture by pretending to be mad. Jewish tradition links Psalm 34 to that episode in his life.   (1 Samuel 21:14)   At one point in his ministry, Jesus was so overworked that he was finding it impossible to eat. "When his relatives heard of this they set out to seize him, for they said, 'He is out of his mind.' "   *Mark 3:21*

When you are overtaxed and overworked, how do you keep your sanity? Discuss this problem with Jesus, who had to deal with it often.

Day seven   Psalm 35

Lord, be not far from me!

Dr. Sheila Cassidy was working as a British surgeon in Chile in 1975. She made the mistake of treating a fugitive from the tyrannical secret police. They arrested her, interrogated her, and tortured her. Meditation on Jesus' suffering and recourse to daily prayer gave her the strength to retain her sanity through eleven weeks of imprisonment. At the end of the ordeal, she understood better the meaning of Psalm 35.

ight, O LORD, against those who fight me;
war against those who make war upon me.
Say to my soul,
"I am your salvation."

O LORD, how long will you look on?
Save me from the roaring beasts.
You, O LORD, have seen; be not silent;
LORD, be not far from me!

Awake, and be vigilant in my defense.
Do me justice, because you are just.
Then my tongue shall recount your justice,
your praise, all the day.   (1, 3, 17, 22–23, 24, 28)

Jesus, too, knew the affront of unjust arrest, the terror of interrogation, and the agony of torture. He knew the ferocity of humans turned into roaring beasts.   (John 19:1–3)

How do you respond when you are unjustly accused? Treated cruelly by others? Speak to Jesus about his suffering and death.

Day one   Psalm 36

You are the source of life, O Lord.

Author Ardis Whitman recalls attending a circus in her childhood. She was amazed by the trapeze artists. Suddenly she turned to her mother and said, "Aren't they afraid?" A man sitting in the row ahead of them turned and said, "Honey, they're not afraid; they trust each other." It was this kind of trust that Israel had in her covenant God.

> O LORD, your kindness reaches to heaven;
> your faithfulness, to the clouds.
> Your justice is like the mountains of God;
> your judgments, like the mighty deep.
>
> How precious is your kindness, O God!
> The children of men take refuge
> in the shadow of your wings.
> They have their fill of the prime gifts
> of your house;
> from your delightful stream you give them to drink.
>
> For with you is the fountain of life,
> and in your light we see light.
> Keep up your kindness toward your friends,
> your just defense of the upright of heart.   (6-7, 8-11)

Jesus said to the official whose daughter was sick, "Do not be afraid; just have faith."   *Mark 5:36*

Recall a time when you found your faith or trust in God tested severely. Why do you think God allowed you to be tested like this? Speak to God about the episode.

The mouth of the just man murmurs wisdom.

In 1947 an Arab teenager found a jar in a cave near the Dead Sea. It contained a two-thousand-year-old biblical scroll. The first of many "Dead Sea Scrolls" found in other caves, it once belonged to a community of Jews who lived just before Jesus. They had gone into the desert to preserve their faith in the face of an evil world. Other scrolls revealed that Psalm 37 held a special meaning for the community.

Trust in the LORD and do good,
that you may dwell in the land
and enjoy security.
Take delight in the LORD,
and he will grant you your heart's requests.

Commit to the LORD your way;
trust in him, and he will act.
He will make justice dawn for you like the light;
bright as the noonday shall be your vindication.

The mouth of the just man tells of wisdom
and his tongue utters what is right.
The law of his God is in his heart,
and his steps do not falter.   (3-6, 30-31)

Some think John the Baptist belonged to the community of Jews, mentioned above, who had gone into the desert to preserve their faith. In any event, he began a reform in the evil world that they had fled.

Do you ever grow discouraged at all the evil in the world? Do you ever wonder why God permits so much evil? Speak to Jesus about these things.

Forsake me not, O Lord.

The person in this psalm is afflicted with a terrible malady, perhaps leprosy, which many ancients regarded as a punishment from God. If we were to search for a modern comparison, we might recall how some people regarded the early victims of the AIDS virus. In any event, the afflicted person cries out from the depths of an anguished soul.

O LORD, in your anger punish me not,
in your wrath chastise me not.
There is no health in my flesh
because of your indignation;
there is no wholeness in my bones.

Noisome and festering are my sores
because of my folly.
My friends and my companions
stand back because of my affliction;
my neighbors stand afar off.

Indeed, I acknowledge my guilt;
I grieve over my sin.
Forsake me not, O LORD;
my God, be not far from me!
Make haste to help me,
O LORD my salvation!　(2, 4, 6, 12, 19, 22–23)

A leper came to Jesus and said, "If you wish, you can make me clean." Jesus said to him, "I do will it. Be made clean." *Mark 1:40–41*

Recall a time when you felt deep anguish of heart over some personal problem or affliction. Speak to Jesus about the compassion he has for afflicted people.

Hear my prayer, O Lord.

Gertrude Ederle dove into the French sea. Her destination was England. Fourteen hours and thirty-one minutes later, she emerged from the water. She had just swum the English Channel faster than any human had ever done. Europe fell at her feet; New York went wild over her. Years later, Gertrude reflected on her hour of glory this way: "When they gave a parade for me, others who had been there before my time watched it. Now I'm watching parades for newcomers to fame. Now I belong to the list of champions-that-were." Gertrude Ederle saw the fleeting nature of fame, much as the psalmist saw the fleeting nature of life.

Let me know, O LORD, my end
and what is the number of my days,
that I may learn how frail I am.

A short span you have made my days,
and my life is as naught before you;
only a breath is any human existence.

Hear my prayer, O LORD;
to my cry give ear.
For I am but a wayfarer before you,
a pilgrim like all my fathers. (5-6, 13)

A rich man stored up wealth for years to come. But God said to him, "You fool, this night your life will be demanded of you." *Luke 12:20*

Recall an "hour of glory" in your life that few people now remember. Speak to Jesus about what really counts in life.

Day five   Psalm 40

Lord, come to my aid!

Actress Helen Hayes will never forget the invasion of France in World War II. Her husband was a part of it. She says in *A Gathering of Hope:* "Unable to sleep, I took my book of psalms and searched for the Ninety-third. Somehow my glance fell on this instead, the Fortieth. The idea of God inclining unto me [stooping toward me] has been from that night on a constant source of hope."

I have waited, waited for the LORD,
*   and he stooped toward me and heard my cry.*
*   He drew me out of the pit of destruction,*
out of the mud of the swamp;
He set my feet upon a crag;
*   he made firm my steps.*

And he put a new song into my mouth,
*   a hymn to our God.*
Many shall look on in awe
*   and trust in the LORD.*

Though I am afflicted and poor,
*   yet the LORD thinks of me.*
You are my help and my deliverer;
*   O my God, hold not back!*   (2–4, 18)

Jesus said, "Ask and you will receive; seek and you will find."   *Luke 11:9*

Recall a time when you turned to God for help in a desperate situation. Speak to Jesus about the various ways his Father answers our prayers.

Lord, heal my soul, for I have sinned against you.

John F. Kennedy said, "If a free society cannot help the many who are poor, it cannot save the few who are rich." And a Jewish proverb says, "Who closes his ear to the poor shall himself cry and not be heard." Psalm 41 makes the same point.

Happy is he who has regard
for the lowly and the poor;
in the day of misfortune
the LORD will deliver him.
The LORD will keep and preserve him;
he will make him happy on the earth,
and not give him over to the will of his enemies.

The LORD will help him on his sickbed,
he will take away all his ailment when he is ill.
Once I said, "O LORD, have pity on me;
heal me, though I have sinned against you."

But because of my integrity you sustain me
and let me stand before you forever.
Blessed be the LORD, the God of Israel,
from all eternity and forever. Amen. Amen.

(2–5, 13–14)

If you say to the needy, " 'Go in peace, keep warm, and eat well,' but you do not give them the necessities of the body, what good is it? So also faith of itself, if it does not have works, is dead." *James 2:16–17*

How "alive" is your faith? Speak to Jesus about how open your own heart is to the cry of the poor.

Day *seven* Psalm 42

My soul is thirsting for the living God.

A chance remark in a Beacon Hill bar led screenwriter Dan Wakefield back to church after years of absence. Describing his return, in the *New York Times Magazine,* he said, "The practice of regular attendance at Sunday services, which such a short time ago seemed religiously 'excessive,' no longer seemed enough. Whatever it was I was getting from church on Sunday morning, I wanted—needed . . . more of it. I experienced what is a common phenomenon for people who . . . begin a journey of the kind I so unexpectedly found myself on—a feeling simply and best described as a 'thirst . . . for God.' "

As the hind longs for the running waters,
so my soul longs for you, O God.

Athirst is my soul for God, the living God.
When shall I go and behold the face of God?

I went with the throng
and led them in procession to the house of God,

Amid loud cries of joy and thanksgiving,
with the multitude keeping festival. (2-3, 5)

"On the last and greatest day of the feast, Jesus stood up and exclaimed, 'Let anyone who thirsts come to me and drink.' " *John 7:37*

To whom or to what do you turn when you thirst for something and don't know what it is? Speak to Jesus about what he gives to those who thirst.

For reflection or discussion

INTRODUCTION Name and describe the five groups into which some people divide the psalms. How would you classify Psalm 29? Psalm 32? Psalm 35?

WEEK 5

1 Surrender

Explain: "Who abandons oneself to God will never be abandoned by God." *Anonymous*

Recall a time when you said to God, "Thy will be done," and really meant it. Why did you do this?

What is something you have your heart set on and find it hard to say to God about it, "Thy will be done"? Why is your heart so set on this one thing?

2 Repentance

Explain: "There are two kinds of repentance: one is that of Judas, the other that of Peter; the one is ice broken, the other ice melted." *William Nevins*

Recall a sin or mistake in your life that you would like to "undo." Why do you regret it so much?

How do you show true repentance for a sin, like cheating or hurting someone?

WEEK 6

1 Trust

Explain: "The more we depend on God, the more dependable we find him." *Cliff Richards*

Recall a time when you trusted someone even though you had misgivings about him or her. Why did you trust the person anyway, and what was the result?

What is a situation in your life right now that calls for trust, either in God or in another person? What tempts you to withhold your trust?

2 Faith

Explain: "If we believe in absurdities, we shall commit atrocities." *Francois Marie Voltaire*

Recall a time when your faith in God flickered and went out (or almost went out). What caused the problem? How did you resolve it?

What is one dimension of your faith that you are having difficulty with right now? What is the cause of this difficulty?

Poetry of
the Psalms

4 *Poetry is a search for syllables
to shoot at the barriers
of the unknown and the unknowable.*
Carl Sandburg

There is poetry in the sight of a shadow falling on a painted wall. The more intricately shaped the shadow, the more beautiful the poetry.

"When power leads man toward arrogance, poetry reminds him of his limitations. When power narrows the area of man's concern, poetry reminds him of the richness and diversity of existence. When power corrupts, poetry cleanses."

Ancient Hebrews would have applauded these words of John F. Kennedy, which he used to dedicate the Robert Frost Library at Amherst College. They, too, had a deep appreciation of the spiritual power of poetry. Nowhere is this more evident than in the psalms.

This chapter examines the psalms from the viewpoint of their structure. The next chapter deals with their imagery.

Unlike English poets, Hebrew poets did not use sound rhyme. Rather, they used thought rhyme, which means they related two lines in a variety of ways. Consider a few examples.

First, Hebrew poets related two lines by repeating, in the second line, the thought expressed in the first line. In other words, the thought in the two lines matched like a pair of shoes. Here is an illustration.

> *Man is like a breath;*
> *his days, like a passing shadow.*   Psalm 144:4

Closer inspection shows that the thought in both lines concerns the *fleeting nature of life on earth.*

A second way that Hebrew poets related two lines was by contrasting the thought of the first line with the thought of the second line.

> *At nightfall, weeping enters in,*
> *but with the dawn, rejoicing.*   Psalm 30:6

Closer study shows that the thoughts of *darkness and sadness* in the first line contrast with the thoughts of *lightness and gladness* in the second line. The two lines are like opposite sides of one coin.

Finally, Hebrews related two lines by completing the thought of the first line in the second line.

> *Unless the Lord guard the city,*
> *in vain does the guard keep vigil.*   Psalm 127:1

These two lines are like two lovers; one without the other is incomplete.

The psalmist did not force every line of every psalm into one of these poetic patterns. On the contrary, he reserved his patterns for strategic points in his psalms.

Needless to say, thought rhyme is not the only device that Hebrew poets used. But it dramatizes an important point. Hebrew poetry is subtle. It reveals itself to the prayerful meditator. It conceals itself from the casual reader.

Hope in God; I will praise him, my savior and my God.

Time magazine described the cell of a priest in Romania. It was damp and totally dark; it reeked of human excrement. The priest said, "I was able at first to get little sleep because rats kept scurrying over me . . . so I passed unforgettable moments of intimate union with the crucifix, which I conjured up in my mind." Psalm 43 reflects the priest's situation.

o me justice, O God, and fight my fight
against a faithless people;
from the deceitful and impious man rescue me.

For you, O God, are my strength.
Why do you keep me so far away?
Why must I go about in mourning,
with the enemy oppressing me?

Send forth your light and your fidelity;
they shall lead me on
And bring me to your holy mountain,
to your dwelling-place.

Then will I go in to the altar of God,
the God of my gladness and joy;
Then will I give you thanks upon the harp,
O God, my God!   (1–4)

Jesus said, "If they persecuted me, they will also persecute you."   *John 15:20*

Recall a time when you suffered for your faith. Speak to Jesus about what good comes from this.

Save us, Lord, in your mercy.

Picture thousands of villagers and farmers running through the gates of the walls that surround Jerusalem. The Judean army has been crushed in battle, and the people are in a state of confusion and panic. Weeping and wailing, they stream into the temple courtyard to pour out their hearts to God.

Yet now you have cast us off
*   and put us in disgrace,*
*   and you go not forth with our armies.*
You have let us be driven back by our foes;
*   those who hated us plundered us at will.*

You made us the reproach of our neighbors,
*   the mockery and the scorn of those around us.*
You made us a byword among the nations,
*   a laughingstock among the peoples.*

Why do you hide your face,
*   forgetting our woe and our oppression?*
For our souls are bowed down to the dust,
*   our bodies are pressed to the earth.* (10–11, 14–15, 25–26)

Jesus said, "Do not be afraid of those who kill the body but after that can do no more. I shall show you whom to fear. Be afraid of the one who after killing has the power to cast into Gehenna; yes, I tell you, be afraid of that one."
Luke 12:4–5

What is the greatest concern you have for the future? For yourself? For our nation? Speak to Jesus about what should be, perhaps, an even greater concern of yours.

Listen to me, daughter;
see and bend your ear.

Picture Jerusalem filled with excitement. The royal wedding is beginning. For months, preparations have been under way. Now the great moment has arrived. The king and royal bride, like every couple in Israel, see their marriage as a covenant with each other, similar to the covenant between God and Israel. This portion of Psalm 45 is addressed to the bride.

Hear, O daughter, and see; turn your ear,
forget your people and your father's house.
*   So shall the king desire your beauty;*
for he is your lord, and you must worship him.

All glorious is the king's daughter as she enters;
*   her raiment is threaded with spun gold.*
In embroidered apparel she is borne in to the king;
*   behind her the virgins of her train*
*   are brought to you.*

They are borne in with gladness and joy;
*   they enter the palace of the king.*
The place of your fathers your sons shall have;
*   you shall make them princes through all the land.*
(11–12, 14–17)

Early Christians saw this psalm as applying to Christ and his bride, the Church.   (Ephesians 5:21–31)

How sacred is the union between man and woman today? Speak to Jesus about how this sacred imagery applies also to Christ and his Church.

Day four   Psalm 46

The mighty Lord is with us;
the God of Jacob is our refuge.

Photographer David Crockett was caught at the foot of Mount Saint Helens when it erupted in 1980. For ten hours he was trapped after being nearly buried alive by millions of tons of falling ash. Miraculously, a helicopter spotted and saved him. "During those ten hours," David said later, "I saw a mountain fall apart. I saw a forest disappear. I saw that God is the only one who is immovable." Then he recalled Psalm 46.

God is our refuge and our strength,
an ever-present help in distress.
Therefore we fear not,
though the earth be shaken
and mountains plunge into the depths of the sea.

There is a stream
whose runlets gladden the city of God,
the holy dwelling of the Most High.
God is in its midst; it shall not be disturbed;
God will help it at the break of dawn.

The LORD *of hosts is with us;*
our stronghold is the God of Jacob.
Come! behold the deeds of the LORD,
the astounding things he has wrought on earth.
(2–3, 5–6, 8–9)

There were times when Jesus thought his world was falling apart, as when his enemies tried to stone him. (John 8:59) Then Jesus, too, turned to prayer.

Recall a time when your world was collapsing around you. How did God help you then? Speak to God about his "ever-present help in distress."

God mounts his throne to shouts of joy; a blare of trumpets for the Lord.

Each year Israel recrowned its king in a kind of anniversary celebration. Scholars suggest the event began with a reenactment of the history of salvation: God's promise to Abraham, God's covenant at Sinai, God's promise of eternal kingship to David's line. Following the reenactment, the king mounted his throne and was recrowned. The celebration ended with a look into the future, when God will mount his throne in heaven and fulfill his promise to bless all nations through Israel.   (Genesis 12:2)

All you peoples, clap your hands,
*   shout to God with cries of gladness,*
*   For the LORD, the Most High, the awesome,*
* is the great king over all the earth.*

God mounts his throne amid shouts of joy;
* the LORD, amid trumpet blasts.*
Sing praise to God, sing praise;
* sing praise to our king, sing praise.*

For king of all the earth is God;
* sing hymns of praise.*
God reigns over the nations,
* God sits upon his holy throne.*   (2-3, 6-9)

Early Christians saw this psalm fulfilled in Christ, when he ascended to his Father to reign in heaven as king of all creation.

Does Christ reign in your heart the way he reigns in heaven? Speak to Jesus about this.

God upholds his city for ever.

Ancients believed in the existence of a great mountain in the far "recesses of the North." It soared above the clouds into heaven itself. Atop the mountain lived the gods. Israel appropriated this image and applied it to the mount on which Jerusalem ("the city of our God") was built. The city's highest point was called Mount Zion, upon which the Temple was built. From the Temple "the great King" guarded the defense towers ("castles") atop the city's walls.

*G*reat is the LORD and wholly to be praised
   in the city of our God.
   His holy mountain, fairest of heights,
   is the joy of all the earth;

Mount Zion, "the recesses of the North,"
   is the city of the great King.
God is with her castles;
   renowned is he as a stronghold.

O God, we ponder your kindness
   within your temple.
As your name, O God, so also your praise
   reaches to the ends of the earth.
Of justice your right hand is full.   (2–4, 10–11)

"I saw the Holy City, the new Jerusalem. . . . I heard a loud voice speaking . . . 'Now God's home is with mankind! . . . There will be no more death, no more grief or crying or pain.' "   *Revelation 21:2–4 (TEV)*

What are you doing to hasten the coming of the "new [spiritual] Jerusalem"? Speak to God about it.

Happy the poor in spirit; the kingdom of heaven is theirs!

Nathaniel Hawthorne once wrote: "A grave, wherever found, preaches a short and pithy sermon to the soul." Psalm 49 preaches a similar sermon.

This is the way of those whose trust is folly,
the end of those contented with their lot:
Like sheep they are herded
into the nether world;
death is their shepherd,
and the upright rule over them.

Quickly their form is consumed;
the nether world is their palace.
But God will redeem me
from the power of the nether world
by receiving me.

Fear not when a man grows rich,
when the wealth of his house becomes great,
For when he dies, he shall take none of it;
his wealth shall not follow him down.

Though in his lifetime he counted himself blessed,
"They will praise you for doing well for yourself,"
He shall join the circle of his forebears
who shall never more see light. (14–20)

"This is how it is with those who pile up riches for themselves but are not rich in God's sight." *Luke 12:21 (TEV)*

Speak to Jesus about what it means to be "rich in God's sight."

To the upright
I will show the saving power of God.

Mel Bitters and his wife were sailing on a lake in Maine. Suddenly a storm blew up, capsizing their boat and blowing it away. Soon they became separated. Mel kept calling to his wife, but got no answer. He thought of the agony of telling their six children, "Mother's dead!" Then he recalled two lines from Psalm 50: "Call upon me in time of distress; I will rescue you." Mel called to God as he had never called before. Minutes later, rescue came for him—and his wife. The seven-hour nightmare was over.

G od the Lord has spoken
and summoned the earth,
from the rising of the sun to its setting.
From Zion, perfect in beauty, God shines forth.

"Gather my faithful ones before me,
those who have made a covenant
with me by sacrifice."
And the heavens proclaim his justice;
for God himself is the judge.

"Offer to God praise as your sacrifice
and fulfill your vows to the Most High;
Then call upon me in time of distress;
I will rescue you, and you shall glorify me."

(1–2, 5–6, 14–15)

"[Jesus] said to the sea, 'Quiet! Be still!' The wind ceased and there was great calm."   *Mark 4:39*

Recall a time when you called out in distress and God saved you. Speak to Jesus about it.

Be merciful, O Lord, for we have sinned.

Young Tom Merton was traveling in Europe, leading a wayward life. One night in his room he had a soul-stirring experience. He says, "I was overwhelmed with a profound insight into the misery and corruption of my soul. . . . And now I think for the first time in my whole life I really began to pray."

Have mercy on me, O God, in your goodness;
in the greatness of your compassion
wipe out my offense.
Thoroughly wash me from my guilt
and of my sin cleanse me.

For I acknowledge my offense,
and my sin is before me always:
"Against you only have I sinned,
and done what is evil in your sight."

A clean heart create for me, O God,
and a steadfast spirit renew within me.
Cast me not out from your presence,
and your holy spirit take not from me.

Give me back the joy of your salvation,
and a willing spirit sustain in me.
O LORD, open my lips,
and my mouth shall proclaim your praise.

(3–6, 12–14, 17)

Jesus said, "I tell you, there will be rejoicing among the angels of God over one sinner who repents." *Luke 15:10*

Recall a time when you had an experience similar to Merton's. Speak to Jesus about God's forgiveness.

1 trust in the kindness of God for ever.

Two boys were returning home from boarding school. They had just taken their first semester exams and were talking about cheating. The older boy boasted that he cheated all the time and made no apologies for it. When the younger boy challenged him, the older boy ridiculed him, saying, "Wise up, stupid, everyone cheats! If you don't look out for yourself, no one else will, not even God!" The psalmist seems to have had someone like the older boy in mind when he lamented:

You love evil rather than good,
falsehood rather than honest speech.
You love all that means ruin.
God himself shall demolish you.

But I, like a green olive tree
in the house of God,
Trust in the kindness of God
forever and ever.

I will thank you always for what you have done,
and proclaim the goodness of your name
before your faithful ones. (5-6, 7, 10-11)

Jesus warned his disciples, "All who take the sword will perish by the sword." *Matthew 26:52*

How honest and trustful are you in your own dealings? How do you respond when someone ridicules you for espousing virtues that are no longer valid in a "dog–eat–dog world"? Speak to Jesus about this.

Day four　　　　　Psalm 53

Oh, that out of Zion would come the salvation of Israel!

A young lawyer was representing a prestigious manufacturing company. A woman had brought suit against the giant firm for an injury received on the job. The lawyer's investigation turned up information that would have strengthened the woman's case considerably. He deliberately suppressed it, however, arguing, "It was my first case, and I wanted to win it." It was concerning people of this stripe—people who trample on the weak and exploit the powerless—that the psalmist cried out to God:

Will all these evildoers never learn,
they who eat up people
just as they eat bread,
who call not upon God?

Oh, that out of Zion would come
the salvation of Israel!
When God restores the well-being of his people,
then shall Jacob exult and Israel be glad. (5, 7)

Jesus sat down and began to preach to the poor and powerless: "Blessed are they who hunger and thirst for righteousness, for they will be satisfied." *Matthew 5:6*

How deeply do you hunger and thirst for justice in today's world? Do you contribute to the injustice in any way? Speak to Jesus about injustice in the world and what you can do to combat it.

Day five   Psalm 54

God himself is my help.

In October 1945, Branch Rickey signed Jackie Robinson as the first black athlete in the big leagues. Before the contract was inked, Rickey told Jackie, "You will have to take everything they dish out and never strike back." Rickey was right. Pitchers brushed him back, and opponents insulted him. Through it all, Jackie kept his cool. In 1947 he was named baseball's Rookie of the Year. In 1949 Jackie won the league's batting championship. In 1961 he was elected to the Hall of Fame. In the midst of his struggle, Jackie might well have prayed these words of Psalm 54.

> *O God, by your name save me,*
> *and by your might defend my cause.*
> *O God, hear my prayer;*
> *hearken to the words of my mouth.*
> *Fierce men seek my life;*
> *they set not God before their eyes.*
>
> *Behold, God is my helper;*
> *the Lord sustains my life.*
> *Freely will I offer you sacrifice;*
> *I will praise your name, O Lord, for its goodness,*
> *Because from all distress you have rescued me.*
> (3–4, 5–6, 8–9)

Jesus said, "Pray for those who mistreat you. To the person who strikes you on one cheek, offer the other one as well."   *Luke 6:28–29*

Speak to Jesus about how his teaching to "turn the other cheek" helped open the door to black athletes in American sports.

Throw your cares on the Lord, and he will support you.

George Washington was extremely sensitive, especially to criticism. In a letter to his wife, Martha, he wrote: "You can imagine my feelings as I reread Thomas Paine's last letter to me. He and I were once friends. As his friend, I tried to get the Virginia legislature to vote him a pension or grant of land. And yet, because I did not think him qualified to become postmaster general, he charged me with being treacherous in private friendship."

If an enemy had reviled me,
I could have borne it;
If he who hates me had vaunted himself
against me,
I might have hidden from him.

But you, my other self,
my companion and my bosom friend!
You, whose comradeship I enjoyed;
at whose side I walked in procession
in the house of God!

But I will call upon God,
and the Lord will save me.
Never will he permit the just man
to be disturbed.   (13–15, 17, 23)

Jesus, too, experienced the pain of being denied and betrayed by those close to his heart.

How do you respond when you are hurt by a friend? Speak to Jesus about how he handled such pain.

Day *seven*   Psalm **56**

I will walk in the presence of God, with the light of the living.

In his youth John Newton went to sea, left his faith, and became a slave trader. One night a storm threatened to destroy his ship. John prayed for the first time in years, promising to mend his ways. When he was spared, John left the slave trade and studied for the ministry. Eventually he was ordained and composed a hymn to celebrate his personal conversion. A part of it reads: "Amazing grace! how sweet the sound, / That saved a wretch like me! / I once was lost, but now am found— / Was blind, but now I see."

N ow I know that God is with me.
In God, in whose promise I glory,
in God I trust without fear;
what can flesh do against me?

I am bound, O God, by vows to you;
your thank offerings I will fulfill.
For you have rescued me from death,
my feet, too, from stumbling;
that I may walk before God
in the light of the living.   (10–14)

"[Jesus] rebuked the wind and said to the sea, 'Quiet! Be still!' The wind ceased and there was great calm." *Mark 4:39*

Retrace the path of your own relationship with Jesus. Speak to him about your hopes for its future.

For reflection or discussion

INTRODUCTION What rhyme scheme did Hebrew poets use? Give an example of rhyme by repetition in Psalm 44; rhyme by contrast (verses) in Psalm 52; rhyme by completion in Psalm 55.

WEEK 7

1   Courage

Explain: "Courage is fear that has said its prayers."
Anonymous

Recall a time when you were truly afraid. What triggered the fear, and how did you deal with it?

What frightens you most about today's world? Why this? What can you do about it?

2   Spouses/Parents

Explain: "It is easier for a father [or a mother] to have children than for children to have a father [or a mother]."
Pope John XXIII

Recall one of the most pleasant memories you have of your spouse or of a parent.

If you could change one thing in your spouse (or your parents), what would it be? Why this?

WEEK 8

1   Honesty

Explain: When asked why she fired her maid, a woman said, "I caught her stealing one of my good Waldorf-Astoria Hotel towels."

Recall a time when you overcame a temptation to steal or cheat. What was your motivation to do so?

Why is there so much dishonesty today? Why do you still believe "Honesty is the best policy"?

2   Friends

Explain: "Anyone can stand up to his opponents; give me someone who can stand up to friends."   *William Gladstone*

Recall a friendship that you failed to maintain and now regret losing. Would it be possible and advisable to reactivate it?

What three things do you look for in a friend? Why these?

Imagery of
the Psalms

5 *Painting is silent poetry;
Poetry is vocal painting.*

Simonides of Ceos

Marc Chagall was one of the greatest artists of the twentieth century. He once said: "When I finish a picture, I hold some God-made object up to it—a rock, a flower, a branch of a tree or my hand—as a kind of final test. If the painting stands up beside a thing man cannot make, the painting is authentic. If there's a clash between the two, it's bad art."

When you study the word pictures in the psalms, you get the feeling that the psalmist did what Chagall did. His images ring true to life. There is no clash between the picture the psalmist paints and the feeling that you have in your heart. The psalms are good art. Consider a few examples.

Psalm 69 is the prayer of an afflicted person experiencing profound anguish and helplessness.

*Save me, O God,
    for the waters threaten my life;
I am sunk in the abysmal swamp
    where there is no foothold;
I have reached the watery depths;
    the flood overwhelms me.*

73

> *I am wearied with calling,*
> *my throat is parched.*   Psalm 69:2-4

The imagery of those lines is clearly that of a person in spiritual agony. They recall times in our own lives when our spirits flickered and almost died.

By way of contrast, consider Psalm 104. It is the prayer of an ecstatic person, wrapped in spiritual excitement as he contemplates his Lord and God.

> *O Lord, my God, you are great indeed!*
> *You are clothed with majesty and glory,*
>   *robed in light as with a cloak.*
> *You make the clouds your chariot.*
> *You make the winds your messengers.*
> *I will sing to the Lord all my life;*
>   *I will sing praise to my God.*   Psalm 104:1-2, 3, 4, 33

Again, the imagery of those lines speaks of ecstasy and jubilation. It recalls times in our own lives when our spirits soared beyond the clouds.

Finally, consider Psalm 23. It is the prayer of a person filled with faith and trust as he walks hand in hand with his loving Lord.

> *The Lord is my shepherd.*
> *He guides me in right paths*
>   *for his name's sake.*
> *Even though I walk in the dark valley*
>   *I fear no evil; for you are at my side*
> *With your rod and your staff*
>   *that give me courage.*   Psalm 23:1, 3-4

Again, the imagery is that of childlike trust in God, a trust that we have all enjoyed at times.

The imagery of the psalms is indeed special. It has one foot on earth and the other foot in heaven, and sometimes it is difficult to say which is where.

Day one   Psalm 57

I will praise you among the nations, O Lord.

Dietrich Bonhoeffer was a Lutheran pastor who was executed by the Nazis in 1945. Just before sunrise on the morning of his execution, Bonhoeffer was taken from his cell and the verdict of the court martial read to him. He was then returned to his cell to make final preparations for his execution. The prison doctor describes what happened next: "I saw Pastor Bonhoeffer . . . kneeling on the floor, praying fervently to his God. I was most deeply moved by the way this lovable man prayed. . . . In the almost fifty years that I worked as a doctor, I have hardly ever seen a man die so entirely submissive to the will of God." Imagine Bonhoeffer praying these words:

My heart is steadfast, O God;
my heart is steadfast;
I will sing and chant praise.
Awake, O my soul; awake, lyre and harp!
I will wake the dawn.

I will give thanks to you among the peoples,
O Lord,
I will chant your praise among the nations.
Be exalted above the heavens, O God;
above all the earth be your glory!   (8–10, 12)

Jesus, too, died totally submissive to the will of his Father, praying, "Father, into your hands I commend my spirit." *Luke 23:46*

Try to imagine the hour of your own death. Say to Jesus now what you would like to say to him then.

There is a God who is judge on earth.

A twenty-five-year-old policeman was attacked as he wrote out a traffic ticket in an area of Dallas that is hostile to police. The assailant grabbed the gun from the officer's holster, and "one or two people" in the crowd cheered and encouraged the man to shoot the policeman. He shot the officer three times in the face. After the shooting, "some in the crowd" told the man to flee; no one helped the officer at any time. Psalm 58 reflects the outrage many citizens felt toward the assailant and the crowd. The imagery of the psalm is foreign to our thinking, but the feeling is not. Referring to incredibly evil people, the psalmist cries out in uncontrollable anguish:

O God, smash their teeth in their mouths.
Let them vanish like water flowing off.
Let them dissolve like a melting snail,
like an untimely birth that never sees the sun.

Unexpectedly, like a thorn-bush,
or like thistles, let the whirlwind
carry them away.

The just man shall be glad.
And men shall say,
"Truly there is a God who is judge on earth!"

(7, 8, 9–11, 12)

Jesus also felt outrage when he saw men turning his Father's house into a market. (John 2:15)

What outrages you in today's world? Speak to Jesus about what keeps you from turning your outrage into constructive action.

Day three   Psalm 59

God is my refuge on the day of distress.

Geoffrey Bull belongs to the long line of heroes who have been imprisoned for their religious or their political beliefs. In his book *When Iron Gates Yield,* he credits his survival in prison to Scripture and prayer. He found it easy to pray Psalm 59.

*R*escue me from my enemies, O my God;
    from my adversaries defend me.
    For behold, mighty men come together against me.
Not for any offense or sin of mine, O LORD.

O my strength! for you I watch;
    for you, O God, are my stronghold,
    my gracious God!
May God come to my aid.

But I will sing of your strength
    and revel at dawn in your kindness;
You have been my stronghold,
    my refuge in the day of distress.

O my strength! your praise will I sing;
    for you, O God, are my stronghold,
    my gracious God!   (2, 4, 10–11, 17–18)

Jesus said, "Come . . . for I was . . . in prison and you visited me." *Matthew 25:34, 35, 36*

Imagine you are unjustly imprisoned in a foreign country. You are totally dependent on groups like Amnesty International for justice and support. Speak to Jesus about why you favor/disfavor such groups.

Help us with your right hand, O Lord, and answer us.

Veterans call it "the wall." The wall's black granite contains the names of 58,132 dead—"inscribed in the order that they were taken from us." "At the age of twenty," wrote one Vietnam vet, "I was put in charge of a riverboat. Now every time I get on a boat, I see only the red blood running over the deck and into the water." Vietnam was a tragic experience for thousands of young soldiers. Many times they felt like the psalmist when he wrote:

> *O God, you have rejected us*
> *and broken our defenses;*
> *you have been angry; rally us!*
>
> *You have rocked the country and split it open;*
> *repair the cracks in it, for it is tottering.*
> *You have made your people feel hardships;*
> *you have given us stupefying wine.*
>
> *Have not you, O God, rejected us,*
> *so that you go not forth, O God, with our armies?*
> *Give us aid against the foe,*
> *for worthless is the help of men.*   (3–5, 12–13)

"There is nothing in all creation that will ever be able to separate us from the love of God which is ours through Christ Jesus our Lord." *Romans 8:39 (TEV)*

What are you doing to promote peace in families? In cities? Among nations? Speak to Jesus, who said, "Blessed are the peacemakers." *Matthew 5:9*

Let me take refuge
in the shelter of your wings.

Two golden cherubim adorned the temple wall. Their outstretched wings touched to form a tentlike shelter. (1 Kings 6:23–28) Thus the expression "in the shelter of your wings" became a popular reference to the Temple. Psalm 61 describes a fugitive (possibly David, 2 Samuel 15–19) longing for the Temple as a trapped lion longs for the hills.

Hear, O God, my cry;
listen to my prayer!
From the earth's ends I call to you
as my heart grows faint.
Oh, that I might lodge in your tent forever,
take refuge in the shelter of your wings!

You indeed, O God, have accepted my vows;
you granted me the heritage
of those who fear your name.
Add to the days of the king's life;
let his years be many generations;

Let him sit enthroned before God forever;
bid kindness and faithfulness preserve him.
So will I sing the praises of your name forever,
fulfilling my vows day by day.   (2–3, 5–9)

Jesus (the new temple, John 2:21) said of Jerusalem, "How many times I yearned to gather your children together, as a hen gathers her young under her wings, but you were unwilling!"   Matthew 23:37

Why do you sometimes refuse to let Jesus take you under his wings? Speak to Jesus about this.

Psalm 62

Rest in God alone, my soul.

Teenager Gary Schneider and two friends got trapped in a blizzard while climbing Mount Hood. They holed up in a snow cave. Sixteen days later, they were down to a daily ration of two spoonfuls of pancake batter. Their sole comfort was the Bible, which one boy had stowed in his backpack. They took turns reading it, eight hours a day. The psalms, especially, gave them support, in particular Psalm 62.

O nly in God is my soul at rest;
from him comes my salvation.
He only is my rock and my salvation,
my stronghold; I shall not be disturbed at all.

Only in God be at rest, my soul,
for from him comes my hope.
He only is my rock and my salvation,
my stronghold; I shall not be disturbed.

With God is my safety and my glory,
he is the rock of my strength;
my refuge is in God.
Trust in him at all times, O my people!
Pour out your hearts before him.   (2–3, 6–9)

Jesus said, "Are not five sparrows sold for two small coins? Yet not one of them has escaped the notice of God. . . . Do not be afraid. You are worth more than many sparrows."   *Luke 12:6–7*

Recall a time when you had to put all your trust in God. Speak to Jesus about his ability to trust.

My soul is thirsting for you,
O Lord my God.

A reporter saw a Bible on General Patton's bedside table. He asked, "Do you read the Bible, General?" Patton replied, "Every goddam night!" Patton's favorite psalm was Psalm 63, which David is said to have prayed in the desert. This psalm was read at Patton's graveside when he was buried on a rainy, fog-shrouded December morning in 1945 at the American Military Cemetery in Luxembourg.

O God, you are my God whom I seek;
for you my flesh pines and my soul thirsts
like the earth, parched, lifeless
and without water.

Thus have I gazed toward you in the sanctuary
to see your power and your glory,
For your kindness is a greater good than life;
my lips shall glorify you.

Thus will I bless you while I live;
lifting up my hands, I will call upon your name.
As with the riches of a banquet
shall my soul be satisfied,
and with exultant lips my mouth shall praise you.

(2–6)

The psalmist speaks of praying and blessing with uplifted hands. Jesus also seems to have prayed and blessed this same way.   (Luke 24:50)

What role does your body play in prayer? Do you ever lift your eyes or arms to heaven? Pray out loud? Talk to Jesus about the value of these things.

The just man is glad in the Lord.

A man was seated at a window, watching a fly crawling across the windowpane. Suddenly a lizard appeared on the other side of the windowpane. It stretched out its tongue to snatch the insect, but the fly remained undisturbed. It sensed it was protected by the windowpane. "That windowpane," the man said, "reminded me of God. He's always there to guard us from those who would harm us." The psalmist had something like this in mind when he wrote:

Hear, O God, my voice.
Shelter me against the council of malefactors.
They devise a wicked scheme,
and conceal the scheme they have devised.

But God brings them down by their own tongues.
And all men fear and proclaim the work of God,
and ponder what he has done.

The just man is glad in the LORD
and takes refuge in him;
in him glory all the upright of heart.   (2, 3, 7, 8, 9, 10–11)

Paul writes, "The Lord is faithful; he will . . . guard you from the evil one."   *2 Thessalonians 3:3*

How trusting are you that God watches over you as a parent watches over a small child? Speak to Jesus about God's personal concern for you.

It is right to praise you in Zion, O God.

A drought struck Israel. Farmers feared for the seed in the dry ground. One by one the watercourses dried up. The specter of famine hung over the land. Prayers went up to God day and night. Then it happened. The rains came just in time. Weeks later, the psalmist looked out across the lush green fields and sang a song of thanksgiving to Yahweh.

ou have visited the land and watered it;
*   greatly have you enriched it.*
*   God's watercourses are filled;*
you have prepared the grain.

Thus have you prepared the land:
*   drenching its furrows,*
*   breaking up its clods,*
Softening it with showers,
*   blessing its yield.*

You have crowned the year with your bounty,
*   and your paths overflow with a rich harvest;*
The untilled meadows overflow with it,
*   and rejoicing clothes the hills.*   (10–13)

One day Jesus looked out across the green fields and said to the people, "If God so clothes the grass in the field that grows today and is thrown into the oven tomorrow, will he not much more provide for you, O you of little faith?" *Luke 12:28*

Recall a time when problems descended on you and God seemed far away. How did the situation resolve itself? Speak to Jesus about your current faith in God and his providence over you.

Day three   Psalm 66

Let all the earth
cry out to God with joy.

The Bible describes Israel's discovery of God. It began
when the Red Sea stood still to let Israel *exit* from Egypt
and climaxed when the Jordan River stood still to let Israel
enter the Promised Land. What happened to Israel happens
to us. We all have our "God-discovery" story. Psalm 66 is
a call to celebrate both "God-discovery" stories: Israel's
and ours.

*S*hout joyfully to God, all you on earth,
    sing praise to the glory of his name;
    proclaim his glorious praise.
Say to God, "How tremendous are your deeds!

"Let all on earth worship and sing praise to you,
    sing praise to your name!"
Come and see the works of God,
    his tremendous deeds among men.

He has changed the sea into dry land;
    through the river they passed on foot;
    therefore let us rejoice in him.
He rules by his might forever.

Hear now, all you who fear God, while I declare
    what he has done for me.
Blessed be God who refused me not
    my prayer or his kindness! (1–3, 4–7, 16, 20)

To find Jesus is to find God. Jesus said, "Whoever has
seen me has seen the Father." *John 14:9*

Review your own "God-discovery" story. Speak to
Jesus about your present relationship with God.

May God bless us in his mercy.

Archaeologists dug into a cave near Jerusalem in 1979. It was filled with jars, oil lamps, and jewelry that dated back to six hundred years before Christ. One object, especially, caught their attention: a tiny silver scroll that once hung around an Israelite's neck. It was inscribed with Aaron's blessing: "The LORD bless you and keep you! The LORD let his face shine upon you, and be gracious to you! The LORD look upon you kindly and give you peace!" *Numbers 6:24–26*   The opening verse of Psalm 67 echoes that beautiful blessing. The remaining verses develop it.

*M*ay God have pity on us and bless us;
may he let his face shine upon us.
So may your way be known upon earth;
among all nations, your salvation.

May the nations be glad and exult
because you rule the peoples in equity;
the nations on the earth you guide.

May the peoples praise you, O God;
may all the peoples praise you!
May God bless us,
and may all the ends of the earth fear him!

(2–3, 5–6, 8)

Jesus embraced the children and "blessed them, placing his hands on them."   *Mark 10:16*

In the play *Brigadoon*, a groom blesses himself before his wedding, saying, "May God bless me as I would he, if I were he and he were me." Talk to God about some special ways he has blessed you.

Psalm **68**

Sing to God, O kingdoms of the earth.

The ark of the covenant was a chest containing the two stone tablets that God gave Moses at Mount Sinai. (1 Kings 8:9)   It localized God's presence among his people. Whenever Israel marched to a new location in the desert, they began with Moses saying to the ark, "Arise, O LORD, that your enemies may be scattered and those who hate you may flee before you."   *Numbers 10:35*   Psalm 68 is a processional hymn that recalls that ancient practice.

G od arises; his enemies are scattered,
and those who hate him flee before him.
As smoke is driven away, so are they driven;
as wax melts before the fire,
so the wicked perish before God.

But the just rejoice and exult before God;
they are glad and rejoice.
Sing to God, chant praise to his name,
extol him who rides upon the clouds,
Whose name is the LORD; exult before him.

The father of orphans and the defender of widows
is God in his holy dwelling.
God gives a home to the forsaken;
he leads forth prisoners to prosperity.   (2-7)

On Palm Sunday a procession escorted Jesus into Jerusalem. "Those preceding him as well as those following kept crying out: 'Hosanna!' "   *Mark 11:9*

Do you let God lead the way for you in life, or do you go your own way? Speak to Jesus about this.

Turn to the Lord in your need, and you will live.

Dorothy Day was a champion of the poor. After her death in 1980, the *New York Times* called her America's most influential Catholic. Describing her weeks of solitary confinement in jail for political protesting in her younger years, she says, "The only thing that brought comfort to my soul was psalms like Psalm 69."

I am sunk in the abysmal swamp
where there is no foothold;
I have reached the watery depths;
the flood overwhelms me.

But I pray to you, O Lᴏʀᴅ,
for the time of your favor, O God!
In your great kindness answer me
with your constant help.

But I am afflicted and in pain;
let your saving help, O God, protect me.
I will praise the name of God in song,
and I will glorify him with thanksgiving.

"See, you lowly ones, and be glad;
you who seek God, may your hearts be merry!
For the Lᴏʀᴅ hears the poor,
and his own who are in bonds he spurns not."

(3, 14, 30–31, 33–34)

"They bound Jesus, led him away, and handed him over to Pilate, the governor." *Matthew 27:2*

Recall a time when you felt like the psalmist and Dorothy Day. Speak to Jesus about it.

Psalm 70

O Lord, make haste to help me.

A missionary writes from Africa: "Many of the children miss school . . . because they have to go to the woods to search for food." Protracted hunger in tiny children causes the belly to swell. Next, the hair turns gray. Then, the skin cracks crazily. Finally, the child dies in mute misery. Africans call this tragic condition *kwashiorkor*. It is the sickness the old baby gets when the new baby comes; there is no mother's milk left for the old baby. The psalmist speaks for these millions of voiceless, starving children when he cries out in anguish:

> *D*eign, O God, to rescue me;
> *O L*ORD*, make haste to help me.*
> *Let them be put to shame and confounded*
> *who seek my life.*
>
> *But may all who seek you*
> *exult and be glad in you,*
> *And may those who love your salvation*
> *say ever, "God be glorified!"*
>
> *O God, hasten to me!*
> *You are my help and my deliverer;*
> *O L*ORD*, hold not back!* (2–3, 5, 6)

The king "will say to those on his left, 'Depart from me. . . . I was hungry and you gave me no food. . . . What you did not do for one of these least ones, you did not do for me.' " *Matthew 25:41–42, 45*

What can Christians do in the face of such a tragic condition? Speak to Jesus about this.

For reflection or discussion

INTRODUCTION What is Marc Chagall's criterion for good art? How does it apply to the psalm images? Check the images in the following psalms and select the three you like best: Psalms 38:9–11; 42:2–5; 51:9–14; 71:17–18; 98:7–8; 102:4–8; 107:23–32; 121:1–2; 139:13–16.

WEEK 9

1 Peace

Explain: After the making of the atom bomb, Albert Einstein said, "Everything is now changed except our attitudes."

Recall a time when you put into practice Jesus' words, "Blessed are the peacemakers, for they will be called children of God." *Matthew 5:9*

Where do you begin to work for peace in the world? Explain.

2 Prayer

Explain: "When the heart begins to recite, the tongue should stop." *Sufi saying* "I have lived to thank God that all my prayers have not been answered." *Jean Ingelow*

Recall a time when you prayed with every fiber of your being.

How, when, where, and how long do you usually pray each day?

WEEK 10

1 Jesus

Explain: "Jesus Christ will be Lord of all or he won't be Lord at all." *Saint Augustine*

When did Jesus first become real for you?

What is one of your favorite parables, miracles, or sayings of Jesus? Explain.

2 Poverty

Explain why this is so: "If a free society cannot help the many who are poor, it cannot save the few who are rich."
John F. Kennedy

Recall a memorable encounter you had with poverty either in your life or the life of another.

What can one person do about poverty? What keeps you from doing this?

The Psalms
and God

6 *Closer is He than breathing,
and nearer than hands and feet.*
Alfred Lord Tennyson

The cloud is often used in the Bible as a symbol of God's presence. God led Israel out of Egypt by means of a cloud. (Exodus 13:21)   God descended on Mount Sinai in a cloud.   (Exodus 19:9)   God filled the Temple with a cloud.   (1 Kings 8:10)   God said from a cloud, "This is my chosen Son."   (Luke 9:35)   God took his Son to heaven in a cloud.   (Acts 1:9)

The cloud is a popular biblical symbol of God's presence. It both reveals and conceals the divine.

The psalms are like the biblical clouds. They too are alive with God. They too pulse with his presence. They too throb with his heartbeat. The writer of Psalm 139 captures the spirit of God's presence in the psalms when he says:

> *Where could I get away from your presence?*
> *If I flew beyond the east*
> *or lived in the farthest place in the west,*
> *you would be there to lead me,*
> *you would be there to help me.*   Psalm 139:7, 9–10 (TEV)

The psalms are like biblical clouds in still another sense. While they reveal God's presence, they also conceal it. They keep the divine masked in mystery. They reveal the thoughts of God's mind, the strength of God's hand, and the depth of God's love; but they conceal the light of his glory. And that is the way it should be. In the psalms we hear the echo of God's words to Moses:

> "I will make all my beauty pass before you. . . . But my face you cannot see. . . . When my glory passes I will set you in the hollow of the rock and will cover you with my hand until I have passed by. Then I will remove my hand, so that you may see my back; but my face is not to be seen." Exodus 33:19-23

And so the psalms both reveal and conceal God's presence. They are not magical doors that afford us passage into the land of the gods. They are doors of faith that afford us passage into the sanctuary of the sacred. And this explains why each day in Israel began with the music of a psalm and ended with the echo of a psalm.

I will sing of your salvation.

Sixty-year-old John Coleman, a former college president, wanted to know what it was like to be a homeless old man in New York City. So, in midwinter, he spent ten days living in the streets. After reading his "Diary of a Homeless Man," you get the feeling that he came to understand Psalm 71.

*I*n you, O LORD, I take refuge;
  let me never be put to shame.
    In your justice rescue me, and deliver me;
  incline your ear to me, and save me.

Be my rock of refuge,
  a stronghold to give me safety,
    for you are my rock and my fortress.
O my God, rescue me from the hand
    of the wicked.

For you are my hope, O LORD;
  my trust, O God, from my youth.
On you I depend from birth;
  from my mother's womb you are my strength.

My mouth shall declare your justice,
  day by day your salvation.
O God, you have taught me from my youth,
  and till the present
    I proclaim your wondrous deeds.   (1-4, 5-6, 15, 17)

"I was . . . a stranger and you gave me no welcome, naked and you gave me no clothing."   *Matthew 25:42-43*

Speak to Jesus about your concern for the homeless.

Lord,
every nation on earth will adore you.

Each new king brought Israel a step closer to the "King of Kings," the promised Messiah. What was said of each new king applied also to the promised Messiah.

O God, with your judgment endow the king,
and with your justice, the king's son;
He shall govern your people with justice
and your afflicted ones with judgment.

Justice shall flower in his days,
and profound peace, till the moon be no more.
May he rule from sea to sea,
and from the River to the ends of the earth.

The kings of Tarshish and the Isles
shall offer gifts;
the kings of Arabia and Seba shall bring tribute.
All kings shall pay him homage,
all nations shall serve him.

For he shall rescue the poor man
when he cries out,
and the afflicted when he has no one
to help him.
He shall have pity for the lowly and the poor;
the lives of the poor he shall save.　　(1-2, 7-8, 10-13)

Jesus said, "The Spirit of the Lord . . . has anointed me to bring glad tidings to the poor."　*Luke 4:18*

Speak to Jesus about his special love for the afflicted, the lowly, and the poor.

Day three   Psalm 73

You have hold of my right hand.

In his *Confessions,* Saint Augustine describes an incident that affected him deeply. He was standing with his mother at a window overlooking a garden. Augustine says: "We had gone there . . . to get away from the noisy crowd and rest. And so the two of us . . . were enjoying a very pleasant conversation. . . . We were asking one another . . . what it would be like to share the eternal life enjoyed by the saints. . . . In the course of our conversation that day, the world and its pleasures lost all attraction for us." Suddenly, Psalm 73 took on new meaning for Augustine.

You have hold of my right hand;
With your counsel you guide me,
and in the end
you will receive me in glory.

Whom else have I in heaven?
And when I am with you,
the earth delights me not.

Though my flesh and my heart waste away,
God is the rock of my heart
and my portion forever.
For me, to be near God is my good.   (23–26, 28)

Jesus said, "In my Father's house there are many dwelling places. . . . If I go and prepare a place for you, I will come back again and take you to myself, so that where I am you may also be." *John 14:2–3*

Speak to Jesus about your thoughts of heaven and your desire to be with him forever.

Lord, forget not
the life of your poor ones.

The fall of Jerusalem and the Temple in 587 B.C. shook the faith of God's people to its foundation. It made them ask themselves a terrifying question.

Why, O God, have you cast us off forever?
Why does your anger smolder
against the sheep of your pasture?
Remember your flock which you built up of old,
the tribe you redeemed as your inheritance,
Mount Zion, where you took up your abode.

Turn your steps toward the utter ruins;
toward all the damage the enemy has done
in the sanctuary.
Your foes roar triumphantly in your shrine;
they have set up their tokens of victory.

They are like men coming up with axes
to a clump of trees;
and now with chisel and hammer
they hack at all its paneling.
They set your sanctuary on fire;
the place where your name abides
they have razed and profaned.   (1–7)

Jesus loved the Temple. How hard it must have been for him to prophesy that the rebuilt Temple would be destroyed again: "There will not be one stone left upon another."   *Mark 13:2*

Why does God let catastrophes happen to us individually and to his people collectively? Speak to Jesus about this vexing question.

Day five   Psalm 75

We give you thanks, O God.

The cup is a popular biblical symbol. Jeremiah 16:7 speaks of comforting someone with the "cup of consolation." Psalm 116:13 speaks of good people drinking from the "cup of salvation." Isaiah 51:17 speaks of sinners drinking from the "cup of God's wrath." It is this latter image that provides the background for understanding the key symbolism in Psalm 75.

We give you thanks, O God, we give thanks,
*   and we invoke your name;*
*   we declare your wondrous deeds.*
God is the judge;
*   one he brings low; another he lifts up.*
For a cup is in the LORD's hand,
*   full of spiced and foaming wine,*
And he pours out from it;
*   even to the dregs they shall drain it;*
*   all the wicked of the earth shall drink.*

But as for me, I will exult forever;
*   I will sing praise to the God of Jacob.*
And I will break off the horns of all the wicked;
*   the horns of the just shall be lifted up.*   (2, 8–11)

Jesus said to James and John, " 'Can you drink the cup of suffering that I must drink?' . . . 'We can,' they answered." *Mark 10:38–39 (TEV)*

Recall a time when you drank from the "cup of suffering." Speak to Jesus about why he suffered.

Resplendent you came, O powerful One.

The prophet Amos tried to get the people to help the poor and the afflicted in their midst. But the people refused. Amos finally passed judgment on them, saying in God's name, "I will deal with you in my own way. . . . Prepare to meet your God, O Israel." *Amos 4:12* And so the fury of God's anger struck. Israel's stouthearted soldiers were despoiled in battle, their steeds slept in death, and their chariots laid in ruins. It is against a background like this that we must read Psalm 76.

esplendent you came, O powerful One,
from the everlasting mountains.
Despoiled are the stouthearted;
they sleep their sleep;
the hands of all the mighty ones have failed.
At your rebuke, O God of Jacob,
chariots and steeds lay stilled.

You are terrible; and who can withstand
the fury of your anger?
From heaven you made your intervention heard;
the earth feared and was silent
When God arose for judgment,
to save all the afflicted of the earth. (5–10)

Jesus said, "Depart from me, you accursed. . . . For I was hungry and you gave me no food." *Matthew 25:41–42*

Speak to Jesus about your own practical concern for the "afflicted of the earth."

I remember the deeds of the Lord.

Some students were given several psalms to read and were asked which one best expressed their present feelings toward God. One boy chose Psalm 77, explaining: "Somewhere in grade school my ideas about God underwent a change. I found myself not taking God seriously. This attitude continued until my sophomore year in high school. Then one Sunday, for a reason I can't explain, I decided to go to church—something I hadn't done since grade school. That Sunday I awoke to a new awareness of God."

I remember the deeds of the LORD;
yes, I remember your wonders of old.
And I meditate on your works;
your exploits I ponder.

O God, your way is holy;
what great god is there like our God?
You are the God who works wonders;
among the peoples
you have made known your power.

With your strong arm
you redeemed your people,
the sons of Jacob and Joseph.
You led your people like a flock
under the care of Moses and Aaron.   (12–16, 21)

One day Jesus told the story of a boy who left home and returned again.   (Luke 15:11–32)

Recall a time when you experienced something similar to what the high school boy did. Speak to God about it.

Day one   Psalm 78

The Lord gave them bread from heaven.

Someone said, "If we lost the Old Testament—except for the Book of Psalms—we could recapture much of the Old Testament story and spirit from the psalms." That's another way of saying that the psalms are a prayerful summary of the spirit of the Old Testament. Psalm 78 is a good illustration of this.

What we have heard and know,
and what our fathers have declared to us,
We will not hide from their sons;
we will declare to the generation to come
The glorious deeds of the LORD and his strength
and the wonders that he wrought.

He commanded the skies above
and the doors of heaven he opened;
He rained manna upon them for food
and gave them heavenly bread.

The bread of the mighty was eaten by men;
even a surfeit of provisions he sent them.
And he brought them to his holy land,
to the mountains his right hand had won.

(3–4, 23–25, 54)

One day at Capernaum, Jesus referred to the event described in this psalm, saying, "Your ancestors ate the manna in the desert, but they died. . . . I am the living bread that came down from heaven; whoever eats this bread will live forever." *John 6:49, 51*

Jesus' words invite you to ask yourself about your own appreciation of Holy Communion. What does it mean to you, personally? Speak to Jesus about this meaning.

For the glory of your name, O Lord, deliver us.

The destruction of Jerusalem and the defilement of the Temple brought all of Israel to its knees. The people cried aloud in anguish to God:

> *O God, the nations have defiled your holy temple,*
> *they have laid Jerusalem in ruins.*
>   *They have given the corpses of your servants*
> *as food to the birds of heaven,*
> *the flesh of your faithful ones*
>   *to the beasts of the earth.*
>
> *They have poured out their blood like water*
>   *round about Jerusalem,*
>   *and there is no one to bury them.*
> *O LORD, how long?*
>   *Will you be angry forever?*
>   *Will your jealousy burn like fire?*
>
> *Remember not against us*
>   *the iniquities of the past;*
>   *may your compassion quickly come to us,*
>   *for we are brought very low.*
>
> *Help us, O God our savior,*
>   *because of the glory of your name;*
> *Deliver us and pardon our sins*
>   *for your name's sake.*   (1–3, 5, 8–9)

Jesus foretold the final fall of the Temple, saying its destruction would be total.   (Mark 13:2)

Speak to Jesus about the meaning that the fall of the Temple and Jerusalem have for you, personally.

The vineyard of the Lord is the house of Israel.

After Solomon's death, a civil war split God's people into two groups: the North, called Israel, and the South, called Judah. In 722 B.C., Assyria invaded the North and enslaved it. The psalmist meditates on Israel's rise and fall, and prays for its restoration.

A vine from Egypt you transplanted;
you drove away the nations and planted it.
It put forth its foliage to the Sea,
its shoots as far as the River.

Why have you broken down its walls,
so that every passer-by plucks its fruit,
The boar from the forest lays it waste,
and the beasts of the field feed upon it?

Once again, O LORD of hosts,
look down from heaven, and see;
Take care of this vine,
and protect what your right hand has planted.

Then we will no more withdraw from you;
give us new life,
and we will call upon your name.
O LORD of hosts, restore us;
if your face shine upon us
then we shall be safe.   (9, 12–16, 19–20)

"Every tree that does not bear good fruit will be cut down and thrown into the fire."   *Matthew 3:10*

If you do not bear good fruit, you too will be lost. Speak to God about the fruit you are bearing.

Day four

I am the Lord, your God:
hear my voice.

The Ten Commandments was one of the most spectacular films ever made. One day a reporter asked its director, Cecil B. DeMille, which commandment people today break most. DeMille said, "The first commandment." He went on to say that people don't worship idols, but they do worship flesh, fame, and fortune. In Psalm 81, God meditates out loud about Israel's failure to keep the first commandment.

There shall be no strange god among you
nor shall you worship any alien god.
I, the LORD, am your God
who led you forth from the land of Egypt.

"But my people heard not my voice,
and Israel obeyed me not;
So I gave them up
to the hardness of their hearts;
they walked according to their own counsels.

"If only my people would hear me,
and Israel walk in my ways,
Quickly would I humble their enemies;
against their foes I would turn my hand."   (10–11, 12–15)

Jesus said, "You shall love the Lord, your God, with all your heart, with all your soul, and with all your mind. This is the greatest and the first commandment."
Matthew 22:37–38

What are some of the "idols" that you worship? Speak to Jesus about why you do this.

Rise up, O God,
bring judgment to the earth.

Someone once said that the only way to view Michelangelo's paintings on the ceiling of the Sistine Chapel in the Vatican is to lie flat on the floor and look straight up. In Psalm 82, the psalmist lies flat on his back, so to speak, and looks straight up to heaven. In his fertile imagination, he sees God passing judgment on those heavenly beings who were supposed to oversee the affairs on earth. Because they have failed in this mission, God condemns them to "die and fall like any prince." God begins his judgment by recalling the instructions he gave them:

efend the lowly and the fatherless;
  render justice to the afflicted and the destitute.
  Rescue the lowly and the poor;
from the hand of the wicked deliver them.

"I said: You are gods,
  all of you sons of the Most High;
Yet like men you shall die,
  and fall like any prince."   (3–4, 6–7)

"Then I saw another angel . . . announce to those who dwell on earth . . . 'Fear God and give him glory, for his time has come to sit in judgment.' "   *Revelation 14:6–7*

How have you carried out God's instructions to show compassion, forgive, comfort, love, and reach out to those in need of help? Speak to Jesus about the accounting you will have to make to God at the end of your life.

O God, be not silent; be not still.

The Holocaust in Nazi Germany in the 1940s caused many Jews to cry, "Where are you, God? Can't you see what's happening? Can't you hear our cries? Don't you see our tears?" But no answer came. God remained silent. God remained still. In biblical times, Jews experienced similar times of trial and suffering. The Holy One who had led them out of Egypt and guided them through the desert appeared to have abandoned them. They too cried out:

O God, do not remain unmoved;
be not silent, O God, and be not still!
For behold, your enemies raise a tumult,
and they who hate you lift up their heads.

Yes, they consult together with one mind,
and against you they are allied.
O my God, make them like leaves in a whirlwind,
like chaff before the wind.

Let them be shamed and put to rout forever;
let them be confounded and perish,
Knowing that you alone are the LORD,
the Most High over all the earth. (2–3, 6, 14, 18–19)

"They crucified Jesus. . . . Those passing by reviled him. . . . And at three o'clock Jesus cried out in a loud voice, . . . 'My God, my God, why have you forsaken me?' " *Mark 15:24, 29, 34*

Recall a time when God appeared not to hear your cries or to see your tears. Speak to Jesus about why God remains silent at certain times in our lives.

Day seven  Psalm 84

Here God lives among his people.

A man was passing the Church of the Little Flower in Royal Oak, Michigan. As he glanced up at the huge crucifix on the front of the church, he saw several birds dancing about on the shoulder of Jesus. Looking closer, he saw that the birds had built a nest between the shoulder of Jesus and the horizontal bar of the cross. He says that episode always comes to mind when he reads Psalm 84.

*My soul yearns and pines
   for the courts of the LORD.
   My heart and my flesh
cry out for the living God.*

*Even the sparrow finds a home,
   and the swallow a nest
   in which she puts her young—
Your altars, O LORD of hosts,
   my king and my God!*

*Happy they who dwell in your house!
   continually they praise you.
Happy the men whose strength you are!
They go from strength to strength.*   (3–6, 8)

"Are not five sparrows sold for two small coins? Yet not one of them has escaped the notice of God. . . . You are worth more than many sparrows." *Luke 12:6–7*

How deeply do you yearn for the presence of the living God? Speak to God about his presence among us and his providence over us.

For reflection or discussion

INTRODUCTION Recall three biblical events in which God's presence was portrayed as a cloud. Why is the cloud an apt symbol of God's presence? In what two ways are the psalms like biblical clouds?

WEEK 11

1   Practical love
Explain: "Love locked in our hearts . . . is like a letter written and not sent."   *Jane Lindstrom*

Recall a time when someone expressed, in a practical way, his or her love for you.

How do you express your love, in a practical way, for the afflicted and the abandoned?

2   Bible reading
Explain: "The Bible is alive, it speaks to me; it has feet, it runs after me; it has hands, it lays hold of me."
Martin Luther

Recall one of your favorite biblical stories or passages. Why is it a favorite?

Why don't you read the Bible more often?

WEEK 12

1   Judgment
Explain: "Do not wait for the last judgment; it takes place every day."   *Albert Camus*

Recall four parables that treat the last judgment. (See Matthew 24:45 and Matthew 25 if you need help.)

What point does Jesus make in each parable?

2   God's presence
Explain: "I sought my soul, but my soul I could not see. I sought my God, but my God eluded me. I sought my brother—and I found all three."   *Anonymous*

Recall a time when you felt God's presence.

Why does God seem to hide his presence from us so often?

The Psalms
and the
New Testament

*7What no man dared to say
was foretold by the psalmist . . .
and afterward
proclaimed by the Lord.*

                                    Saint Ambrose

Bridges are beautiful. They are also practical. They make
it possible for us to cross over from one side of a river to
the other. A world without bridges would be a less lovely,
less livable world.

The psalms are like bridges. They allow us to cross
over from one side of the biblical world to the other. They
let us stand on the Old Testament side of the Bible and
cross over to the New Testament side. What Augustine
said of the entire Bible is especially true of the psalms. "In
the Old Testament the New Testament lies concealed. In
the New Testament the Old Testament lies revealed."

This means that there is more to the psalms than
meets the eye. There is more to them than just the historical
situation to which they primarily refer. There is deeper and
richer significance to be found in them.

For example, no Christian can read the psalms without
marveling at how some of them point to the future Messiah.
The Messiah is not mentioned by name, but his figure is

foreshadowed in many psalms and psalm passages. New Testament writers were the first to apply these psalms to Jesus.

The royal psalms—for example, Psalms 2 and 72—are vivid descriptions of the ideal king. Though these psalms were applied to historical kings, the ideals they set forth can be found only in the Messiah, the "King of Kings."

> *He shall defend the afflicted among the people,*
> *save the children of the poor,*
> *and crush the oppressor.*
> *All kings shall pay him homage,*
> *all nations shall serve him.*
> *May his name be blessed forever;*
> *may the whole earth be filled with his glory.*
> Psalm 72:4, 11, 17, 19

The following are some examples of how New Testament writers applied portions or verses of the psalms to Jesus.

Acts 13:33	*You are my son;* *this day I have begotten you.* Psalm 2:7
Acts 13:35	*Nor will you suffer your faithful one* *to undergo corruption.* Psalm 16:10
John 2:17	*Zeal for your house consumes me.* Psalm 69:10
John 13:18	*Even my friend who partook of my bread,* *has raised his heel against me.* Psalm 41:10
Matthew 21:9	*Blessed is he who comes* *in the name of the LORD.* Psalm 118:26
Matthew 21:42	*The stone which the builders rejected* *has become the cornerstone.* Psalm 118:22

Lord, let us see your kindness.

The fall of Jerusalem in 587 B.C. crushed God's people. For fifty years they were held captive in Babylon. Finally they were freed and returned to rebuild their homeland. But the initial joy of freedom was short-lived. The people found themselves working with one hand and fighting off enemies with the other. They began to wonder if God was still angry with them for the sins of their past. Psalm 85 reflects both the initial joy and the later questioning.

You have favored, O LORD, your land;
you have restored the well-being of Jacob.
You have forgiven the guilt of your people;
you have covered all their sins.
You have withdrawn all your wrath;
you have revoked your burning anger.

Restore us, O God our savior,
and abandon your displeasure against us.
Will you be ever angry with us,
prolonging your anger to all generations?

Will you not instead give us life;
and shall not your people rejoice in you?
Show us, O LORD, your kindness,
and grant us your salvation.   (2-8)

Jesus said, "You will grieve, but your grief will become joy . . . and no one will take your joy away from you." *John 16:20, 22*

Speak to Jesus about why his Father permits his children to suffer so much in this world.

Listen, Lord, and answer me.

Thornton Wilder's novel *The Eighth Day* is about a family who suffers from misfortune and hostility. Yet they never grow bitter or lose their faith in God. The novel ends without the family being rewarded or the villains being punished. Wilder simply suggests that the family's plight is like a tapestry. From the back it looks ugly; from the front, beautiful. That is, from the viewpoint of this world, the family's plight is filled with tragedy; from the viewpoint of the next world, it is filled with glory. The spirit of Wilder's family is the spirit of Psalm 86.

Incline your ear, O Lord; answer me,
for I am afflicted and poor.
Keep my life, for I am devoted to you;
save your servant who trusts in you.

You are my God; have pity on me, O Lord,
for to you I call all the day.
Gladden the soul of your servant,
for to you, O Lord, I lift up my soul;

For you, O Lord, are good and forgiving,
abounding in kindness to all who call upon you.
Hearken, O Lord, to my prayer
and attend to the sound of my pleading. (1–6)

"The sufferings of this present time are as nothing compared with the glory to be revealed for us." *Romans 8:18*

Speak to Jesus about Paul's words and why it is sometimes hard to live by them.

God is with us.

God chose the Jews as his people; he also chose Jerusalem as his holy city. Thus, New Testament writers compared Jerusalem to heaven itself. (Revelation 21:2) And why shouldn't they, for God had filled the Jerusalem Temple with his presence. And so the psalmist sings of God's house in God's city.

His foundations upon the holy mountains
the LORD *loves,*
The gates of Zion,
more than any dwelling of Jacob.
Glorious things are said of you,
O city of God!

I tell of Egypt and Babylon
among those that know the LORD;
Of Philistia, Tyre, Ethiopia:
"This man was born there."
And of Zion they shall say:
"One and all were born in her;
And he who has established her
is the Most High LORD."

They shall note, when the peoples are enrolled:
"This man was born there."
And all shall sing, in their festive dance:
"My home is within you." (1-7)

"I heard a loud voice from the throne saying, 'Behold, God's dwelling is with the human race.' " *Revelation 21:3*

What did Jesus see in the human race that made him dwell with them? Speak to God about this.

Let my prayer come before you, Lord.

Imagine an AIDS victim lying face-to-the-wall in a rundown apartment in Harlem. He has been abandoned by family, by friends, and, it would seem, even by God. Death is approaching. The author of Psalm 88 finds himself in a desperate situation like this.

O LORD, my God, by day I cry out;
at night I clamor in your presence.
Let my prayer come before you;
incline your ear to my call for help,

For my soul is surfeited with troubles
and my life draws near to the nether world.
I am numbered with those
who go down into the pit;
I am a man without strength.

My couch is among the dead,
like the slain who lie in the grave,
Whom you remember no longer
and who are cut off from your care.

You have plunged me into the bottom of the pit,
into the dark abyss.
Upon me your wrath lies heavy,
and with all your billows you overwhelm me.   (2-8)

"There is nothing in all creation that will ever be able to separate us from the love of God which is ours through Christ Jesus our Lord."   *Romans 8:39 (TEV)*

Do you think many people are abandoned, like the psalmist—right now? Speak to God about them.

Day five   Psalm 89

For ever I will sing
the goodness of the Lord.

God's covenant with David is described in 2 Samuel 7. It is the first of a parade of promises that point to a person who, in time, will become known as the *Messiah* ("the Anointed"). The parade of "messianic promises" eventually reaches fulfillment in Jesus. Psalm 89 recalls the inaugural promise. It was a promise that changed the course of human history and gave hope to a despairing world.

I have made a covenant with my chosen one,
I have sworn to David my servant:
Forever will I confirm your posterity
and establish your throne for all generations."

"I have found David, my servant;
with my holy oil I have anointed him,
That my hand may be always with him,
and that my arm may make him strong.

"My faithfulness and my kindness
shall be with him,
and through my name shall his horn be exalted.
He shall say of me, 'You are my father,
my God, the Rock, my savior.' "   (4–5, 21–22, 25, 27)

"The woman [at the well] said to Jesus, 'I know that the Messiah is coming, the one called the Anointed; when he comes, he will tell us everything.' Jesus said to her, 'I am he, the one who is speaking with you.' "   *John 4:25–26*

Imagine you are the woman. What is your reaction to Jesus' revelation? Speak to Jesus about it.

Day six   Psalm 90

In every age, O Lord,
you have been our refuge.

When Jimmy Carter was president, he kept a plaque on his desk. It read: "O God, thy sea is so great and my boat is so small." God's greatness and our smallness is also the theme of Psalm 90.

Before the mountains were begotten
and the earth and the world were brought forth,
from everlasting to everlasting you are God.

You turn man back to dust,
saying, "Return, O children of men."
For a thousand years in your sight
are as yesterday, now that it is past,
or as a watch of the night.

Seventy is the sum of our years,
or eighty, if we are strong,
And most of them are fruitless toil,
for they pass quickly and we drift away.

Fill us at daybreak with your kindness,
that we may shout for joy and gladness
all our days.
Let your work be seen by your servants
and your glory by their children.   (2–4, 10, 14, 16)

"No one could count all the people! . . . They threw themselves face downward . . . and worshiped God, saying, '. . . honor, power, and might belong to our God forever and ever!' "   *Revelation 7:9, 11–12 (TEV)*

Why does this God love you? Why does he care for you? Speak to God about this mystery.

In you, my God, I place my trust.

The famous actor Jimmy Stewart was a pilot in World War II. Before Jimmy left for combat, his father slipped this note into his son's pocket: "Dear Jim, Soon after you read this letter, you will be on your way to the worst sort of danger. . . . I am banking on the enclosed copy of Psalm 91. The thing that takes the place of fear and worry is the promise of these words. . . . I can say no more. . . . I love you more than I can tell you. Dad"

You who dwell in the shelter of the Most High,
who abide in the shadow of the Almighty,
say to the Lord, "My refuge and my fortress,
my God, in whom I trust."

Because he clings to me, I will deliver him;
I will set him on high
because he acknowledges my name.
He shall call upon me, and I will answer him;
I will be with him in distress;

I will deliver him and glorify him;
with length of days I will gratify him
and will show him my salvation.   (1–2, 14–16)

The devil quoted this same psalm to Jesus, urging him to throw himself from the top of the Temple, saying that God would protect him. Jesus refused, saying, "You shall not put the Lord, your God, to the test."   *Luke 4:12*

Recall a time when God helped you in some danger. Speak to God about it and thank him for it.

Lord, it is good to give thanks to you.

Author Stephen McKenna says, "There are trees that are all a-strain upward like a prayer; there are trees that rise only to flow eternally downwards, drooping like death . . . but in all trees there is a beauty." The psalmist agreed. He liked to compare a good person to a tree. The most magnificent of all trees in biblical times was the cedar of Lebanon. It scraped the sky and attained diameters of thirteen feet. Its wood was used to panel the inner walls of the Temple.

It is good to give thanks to the LORD,
to sing praise to your name, Most High,
To proclaim your kindness at dawn
and your faithfulness throughout the night.

The just man shall flourish like the palm tree,
like a cedar of Lebanon shall he grow.
They that are planted in the house of the LORD
shall flourish in the courts of our God.

They shall bear fruit even in old age;
vigorous and sturdy shall they be,
Declaring how just is the LORD,
my Rock, in whom there is no wrong.   (2–3, 13–16)

Jesus was fond of the "tree" image. For example, he compared God's kingdom to a tiny mustard seed that becomes a tree in which the birds of the air make their nests.   (Luke 13:19)

What is there about a tree that makes it a good symbol for a good person? Speak to God about this.

The Lord is king; he is robed in majesty.

Each year Israel's king was recrowned. This practice would remind the king (1) that he had better be worthy of his office or his subjects wouldn't rejoice at his recrowning the next year and (2) that the only eternal king was God, not he. The ceremony of reenthronement would call for joyful celebration: martial music, drum rolls, fanfares, and dancing. Although Psalm 93 is a meditation on the kingship of God, it would have been ideal for a recrowning ceremony. After all, the king was the representative of God, the eternal king.

*The LORD is king, in splendor robed;
   robed is the LORD and girt about with strength;
      And he made the world firm,
   not to be moved.
Your throne stands firm from of old;
   from everlasting you are, O LORD.*

*More powerful than the roar of many waters,
   more powerful than the breakers of the sea—
   powerful on high is the LORD.*

*Your decrees are worthy of trust indeed:
   holiness befits your house,
   O LORD, for length of days.*   (1–2, 4–5)

Pilate said to Jesus, " 'Are you the King of the Jews?' . . . Jesus answered, 'My kingdom does not belong to this world.' "   John 18:33, 36

Does Jesus reign over your heart? Speak to Jesus about the leadership role he plays in your life.

The Lord will not abandon his people.

A bumper sticker reads, "Stop the world; I want to get off!" It echoes how many people feel in the face of mounting crime and brazen exploitation of the poor and the powerless. The psalmist echoes this same feeling but, at the same time, affirms that God is in control and will act at the appropriate time.

Your people, O LORD, they trample down.
Widow and stranger they slay,
the fatherless they murder,
And they say, "The LORD sees not;
the God of Jacob perceives not."
Understand, you senseless ones among the people;
and, you fools, when will you be wise?

Shall he who shaped the ear not hear?
or he who formed the eye not see?
Shall he who instructs nations not chastise,
he who teaches men knowledge?

For the LORD will not cast off his people,
nor abandon his inheritance;
But judgment shall again be with justice,
and all the upright of heart shall follow it.

(5, 6-10, 14-15)

Paul writes: "We must all appear before the judgment seat of Christ, so that each one may receive recompense, according to what he did in the body, whether good or evil." *2 Corinthians 5:10*

Imagine yourself before Christ's judgment seat. Speak to Jesus about your life up to this point.

Day four   Psalm 95

If today you hear his voice,
harden not your hearts.

The Temple had four courts: the *Gentiles' court,* beyond which non-Jews couldn't go; the *women's court,* beyond which women couldn't go; the *men's court,* beyond which men couldn't go; the *priests' court.* Entry into each court was by a gate. Psalm 95 seems to have been part of the liturgy for passing through the gates. "Come, let us sing" signaled permission to enter the first; "Come, let us bow" signaled permission to enter the second ("Beautiful Gate").

C *ome, let us sing joyfully to the LORD;*
*   let us acclaim the Rock of our salvation.*
*   Let us greet him with thanksgiving;*
let us joyfully sing psalms to him.

Come, let us bow down in worship;
*   let us kneel before the LORD who made us.*
For he is our God,
*   and we are the people he shepherds,*
*   the flock he guides.*

O, that today you would hear his voice:
*   "Harden not your hearts as at Meribah,*
*   as in the day of Massah in the desert,*
Where your fathers tempted me;
*   they tested me*
*   though they had seen my works."*   (1–2, 6–9)

A cripple used to sit at " 'the Beautiful Gate' every day to beg for alms." *Acts 3:2*

How reverent are you in God's house? Speak to God about the purpose and value of reverence.

The Lord comes to judge the earth.

Someone said, "To the ancient world, the Jews were a race of madmen. But to the modern world, as we look back, they were the only sane race in a world of madmen. For instead of fearing God's rule and judgment, they rejoiced that it was coming." Psalm 96 illustrates this idea.

*S*ing to the LORD a new song;
sing to the LORD, all you lands.
Tell his glory among the nations;
among all peoples, his wondrous deeds.

For great is the LORD and highly to be praised;
awesome is he, beyond all gods.
For all the gods of the nations
are things of nought,
but the LORD made the heavens.

Let the heavens be glad and the earth rejoice;
let the sea and what fills it resound;
let the plains be joyful and all that is in them!

Then shall all the trees of the forest exult
before the LORD, for he comes;
for he comes to rule the earth.
He shall rule the world with justice
and the peoples with his constancy. (1, 3–5, 11–13)

"Yes, Lord God almighty, your judgments are true and just." *Revelation 16:7*

How do you feel about God's future judgment and rule? Speak to God about it.

A light will shine on us this day: the Lord is born for us.

One of the loveliest Christmas homilies ever preached was by Pope Leo the Great. Part of it reads: "Today our Savior is born; let us rejoice. . . . No one is shut out from this joy; all share the same reason for rejoicing. . . . Let the saint rejoice as he sees the palm of victory at hand. Let the sinner be glad as he receives the offer of forgiveness. Let the pagan take courage as he is summoned to life. . . . And so at the birth of our Lord the angels sing in joy: 'Glory to God in the highest.' . . . What joy Christmas should bring to the lowly hearts of men." This is why many Christmas services include Psalm 97. It speaks prophetically of the Savior's birth.

The Lord is king; let the earth rejoice;
let the many isles be glad.
The heavens proclaim his justice,
and all peoples see his glory.

Light dawns for the just;
and gladness, for the upright of heart.
Be glad in the Lord, you just,
and give thanks to his holy name.   (1, 6, 11–12)

"The angel of the Lord appeared to the shepherds and the glory of the Lord shone around them. . . . And suddenly there was a multitude of the heavenly host with the angel, praising God and saying: 'Glory to God in the highest.' "   *Luke 2:9, 13–14*

Recall an especially joyful Christmas in your life. Speak to Jesus about what made it joyful.

All the ends of the earth
have seen the saving power of God.

Robert Louis Stevenson wrote: "Loving Father, help us remember the birth of Jesus, that we may share in the song of the angels, the gladness of the shepherds, and the worship of the wise men." This is why Christmas services often include Psalm 98.

*S*ing to the LORD a new song,
for he has done wondrous deeds;
His right hand has won victory for him,
his holy arm.

The LORD has made his salvation known:
in the sight of the nations
he has revealed his justice.
He has remembered his kindness
and his faithfulness
toward the house of Israel.

All the ends of the earth have seen
the salvation by our God.
Sing joyfully to the LORD, all you lands;
break into song; sing praise.

Sing praise to the LORD with the harp,
with the harp and melodious song.
With trumpets and the sound of the horn
sing joyfully before the King, the LORD.   (1–6)

"I proclaim to you good news of great joy. . . . A savior has been born for you."   *Luke 2:10–11*

Speak to Jesus about why he became man and what the world would be like had he not done so.

For reflection or discussion

INTRODUCTION Explain Augustine's statement that in the Old Testament the New Testament lies concealed, and in the New Testament the Old Testament lies revealed. Recall some examples of how New Testament writers apply the psalms to Jesus.

WEEK 13

1   Loneliness

Explain: "People are lonely because they build walls instead of bridges."   *J. F. Newton*

Recall a time when you felt lonely or abandoned through no fault of your own.

How do you handle loneliness when it comes?

2   God's providence

Explain: "Behind a frowning providence He hides a shining face."   *William Cowper*

Recall a time when you experienced God's providence in your life in a very special way.

How deeply into our lives do you think God's providence extends?

WEEK 14

1   Reverence

Explain: "I sometimes kneel to feel reverence, not to express it."   *Anonymous*

Recall a time when you were overwhelmed by a reverence for God, either in church or in nature.

Why aren't people as reverent today as they once were?

2   Jesus' birth

Explain: "Welcome, all wonders in one sight! / Eternity shut in a span. / Summer in Winter, Day in Night! / Heaven in earth, and God in man."   *Richard Crashaw*

Recall a happy Christmas. A sad one.

What would be the most different about the world today had Jesus not been born into it?

The Psalms and Jesus

8
In the psalms . . .
Jesus endures his saving passion,
rises, and ascends to heaven.

Saint Ambrose

A world without windows would be like a face without eyes. It would be like a magazine or newspaper without pictures. A windowless world would be a drab world.

What windows are to the world, the psalms are to the Bible. The psalms let us look out onto the colorful landscape of the biblical world. More importantly, they let us look into the hearts of the people who walked around on that landscape. They let us see how these people felt in moments of sorrow, joy, and danger. For the psalms are the prayers these people turned to at those moments.

All of this makes it possible for us to use the psalms as a window into the mind and the heart of Jesus also. For he too prayed these same psalms in times of sorrow, joy, and danger.

Take just one example. If we want to know what went on in the mind and the heart of Jesus as he hung on the cross, we can do no better than read Psalm 22. For Mark and Matthew both tell us that Jesus prayed that psalm on that occasion. (Mark 15:34, Matthew 27:46) Written six hundred years before the Romans devised death by crucifixion, this psalm mirrors Jesus' situation perfectly.

> *My God, my God, why have you forsaken me?*
> *My throat is dried up like baked clay,*
>   *my tongue cleaves to my jaws.*
> *A pack of evildoers closes in upon me;*
>   *they have pierced my hands and my feet.*
> *They divide my garments among them,*
>   *and for my vesture they cast lots.*
> *O LORD, be not far from me;*
>   *O my help, hasten to aid me.*   Psalm 22:1, 16, 17, 19, 20

And if we wanted to know what went on in the mind of Jesus as he made his yearly pilgrimage to the Jerusalem Temple, we could do no better than read Psalm 84. For this was one of the psalms pilgrims prayed on their way to Zion.

> *My soul yearns and pines*
>   *for the courts of the LORD.*
> *My heart and my flesh*
>   *cry out for the living God.*
> *Happy the men whose strength you are!*
>   *their hearts are set upon the pilgrimage.*
> *They shall see the God of gods in Zion.*   Psalm 84:3, 6, 8

The meditations in this book point out other occasions when Jesus probably prayed certain psalms. In the light of this, you may wish to go back, check out some of these psalms, and read them against the background of when Jesus probably prayed them.

Day one   Psalm 99

Holy is the Lord our God.

When you feed a squirrel a nut, its front legs pull toward you and its rear legs pull away from you. Two instincts are in conflict: attraction and fear. Theologian Rudolph Otto says the same is true of people when they encounter God. They experience attraction and fear. To worship the "holy" God means to fall at God's feet in a posture of both attraction and fear. Psalm 99 reflects this strange paradox.

The Lord is king; the peoples tremble;
holy is he.
Extol the Lord, our God,
and worship at his footstool;
holy is he!

Moses and Aaron were among his priests,
and Samuel, among those who called upon
his name;
they called upon the Lord,
and he answered them.

From the pillar of cloud he spoke to them;
they heard his decrees and the law
he gave them.

Extol the Lord, our God,
and worship at his holy mountain;
for holy is the Lord, our God.   (1, 3, 5–7, 9)

Jesus' apostles were both attracted and terrified by what happened on Mount Tabor.   (Mark 9:5–6)

Recall a time when you were both attracted and terrified by something. Speak to God about it.

Come with joy
into the presence of the Lord.

Annabelle Baldwin says in "The Divine Office Can Make Your Day": "All over the world, in convents and monasteries, in rectories and ordinary homes, there are Catholics who greet the dawn with the same prayers. The leather-bound books [they use] are breviaries, and the prayers [mostly psalms] they contain are called the 'Divine Office.' " A popular way people begin their morning prayer is with Psalm 100. A prayerful reading of the psalm shows why it makes a good leadoff prayer.

Sing joyfully to the LORD, all you lands;
serve the LORD with gladness;
come before him with joyful song.

Know that the LORD is God;
he made us, his we are;
his people, the flock he tends.

Enter his gates with thanksgiving,
his courts with praise;

Give thanks to him; bless his name,
for he is good:
the LORD, whose kindness endures forever,
and his faithfulness, to all generations.   (1–4)

"Rising very early before dawn, Jesus left and went off to a deserted place, where he prayed."   *Mark 1:35*

How do you begin your day? Speak to Jesus about why he began his day as he did.

Day three

I will walk with blameless heart.

The winter at Valley Forge in 1777 was a hard time for General George Washington and his army. A staff officer wrote about it later: "The unfortunate soldiers were in want of everything. The army frequently went days without food; and the patient endurance of soldiers and officers was a miracle." When Washington accepted command of the American Revolutionary forces, he prayed Psalm 101.

> *Of kindness and judgment I will sing;*
> *to you, O Lord, I will sing praise.*
> *I will persevere in the way of integrity;*
> *when will you come to me?*
>
> *I will walk in the integrity of my heart,*
> *within my house;*
> *I will not set before my eyes any base thing.*
>
> *Whoever slanders his neighbor in secret,*
> *him will I destroy.*
> *The man of haughty eyes and puffed-up heart*
> *I will not endure.*
>
> *My eyes are upon the faithful of the land,*
> *that they may dwell with me.*
> *He who walks in the way of integrity*
> *shall be in my service.*   (1–3, 5–6)

Before ascending to his Father, Jesus assured his followers, "I am with you always."   *Matthew 28:20*

Do you really believe Jesus is with us always, especially in times of trial? Speak to Jesus about this.

Day four   Psalm 102

From heaven
the Lord looks down on the earth.

Picture a poor Israelite, hundreds of miles from home, doing forced labor in Babylon. His back aches, but his heart aches even more, as he thinks of Jerusalem and the Temple in ruins. Yet he never loses hope. Raising his eyes to heaven, he speaks out loud to God:

You, O LORD, abide forever,
and your name through all generations.
You will arise and have mercy on Zion,
for it is time to pity her.
For her stones are dear to your servants,
and her dust moves them to pity.

And the nations shall revere your name, O LORD,
and all the kings of the earth your glory,
When the LORD has rebuilt Zion
and appeared in his glory;
When he has regarded the prayer of the destitute,
and not despised their prayer.

Let this be written for the generation to come,
and let his future creatures praise the LORD:
"The LORD looked down from his holy height,
from heaven he beheld the earth,
To hear the groaning of the prisoners,
to release those doomed to die."   (13–14, 15–21)

Jesus said, "Come to me, all you who labor and are burdened, and I will give you rest."   *Matthew 11:28*

Think of some of the people in today's world whose backs and hearts ache. Pray to Jesus for them.

The Lord is kind and merciful.

Young Ibrahim ibn Adham was walking alone under the stars. Suddenly he knelt and prayed, "O Lord, let me never stray from you." No sooner had he made his prayer than a voice said, "Ibrahim, if I granted your request, how could I ever show you my mercy?" Psalm 103 extols God's infinite mercy.

*B**less the L**ORD**, O my soul;**
and all my being, bless his holy name.
Bless the LORD**, O my soul,**
and forget not all his benefits;*

He pardons all your iniquities,
he heals all your ills.
He redeems your life from destruction,
he crowns you with kindness and compassion.

He will not always chide,
nor does he keep his wrath forever.
Not according to our sins does he deal with us,
nor does he requite us according to our crimes.

For as the heavens are high above the earth,
so surpassing is his kindness
toward those who fear him.
As far as the east is from the west,
so far has he put our transgressions from us.

(1–4, 9–12)

Jesus said, "Blessed are the merciful, for they shall be shown mercy." *Matthew 5:7*

Recall some things in your life for which God has forgiven you. Speak to God about them.

Day six   Psalm 104

O, bless the Lord, my soul!

Richard Wurmbrand writes in his book *In God's Underground:* "Martin Luther used to raise his hat to the birds and say, 'Good morning, theologians—you wake and sing, but I, old fool, know less than you and worry about everything, instead of simply trusting in the heavenly Father's care.' " Psalm 104 celebrates the trust that God's creatures have in their Creator, who is clothed with majesty and glory.

less the LORD, O my soul!
O LORD, my God, you are great indeed!
You are clothed with majesty and glory,
  robed in light as with a cloak.

[Creatures] all look to you
  to give them food in due time.
When you give it to them, they gather it;
  when you open your hand,
    they are filled with good things.

If you take away their breath, they perish
  and return to their dust.
When you send forth your spirit,
  they are created,
  and you renew the face of the earth.   (1–2, 27–28, 29–30)

Jesus assures us that if his Father in heaven doesn't forget a single bird that flies in the sky, he won't forget us either. (Luke 12:6–7)

Speak to God about why you find it so hard to trust him totally and completely.

Day seven   Psalm 105

Remember the marvels the Lord has done.

George Washington Carver was born a slave. He never knew his father or mother. He never even knew his name. Yet he became a great scientist. From the peanut he made nearly three hundred useful products. From the sweet potato he made over a hundred products. When asked the secret of his success, he said that he used to rise each morning at four o'clock and walk in the woods. "In the woods," he explained, "while most other persons are sleeping, I hear and understand God's plan for me." Psalm 105 held a special meaning for George Washington Carver.

When the LORD called down a famine on the land
and ruined the crop that sustained them,
He sent a man before them,
Joseph, sold as a slave;

They had weighed him down with fetters,
and he was bound with chains,
Till his prediction came to pass
and the word of the LORD proved him true.

The king sent and released him,
the ruler of the people set him free.
He made him lord of his house
and ruler of all his possessions. (16–21)

"Blessed are the poor in spirit, for theirs is the kingdom of heaven. . . . Blessed are the meek, for they will inherit the land." *Matthew 5:3, 5*

Speak to God about why he promised to bless the poor in spirit and the meek so lavishly.

Lord, remember us, for the love you bear your people.

Psalm 106 is another illustration of the remark, "If the Old Testament were lost, except for the Book of Psalms, much of the Bible's story and spirit could be recovered from that book alone." It recalls Israel's escape from Egypt, its covenant with God at Mount Sinai (Horeb), its sinfulness in the desert, and its entrance into the Promised Land (Canaan). The psalm's point is to contrast Israel's infidelity to God with God's fidelity to Israel—in spite of moments when God's righteous anger nearly exploded. One of those explosive moments was the "golden calf" episode.

O ur fathers made a calf in Horeb
and adored a molten image;
They exchanged their glory
for the image of a grass-eating bullock.

They forgot the God who had saved them,
who had done great deeds in Egypt,
Wondrous deeds in the land of Ham,
terrible things at the Red Sea.

Then he spoke of exterminating them,
but Moses, his chosen one,
Withstood him in the breach
to turn back his destructive wrath.   (19–23)

Righteous anger raged in Jesus, also, when he ran the merchants from the Temple.   (John 2:13–17)

How do you keep control of yourself in times of anger? Speak to Jesus about how he controlled anger.

Give thanks to the Lord, his love is everlasting.

Alexander Selkirk, a British sailor, spent four years alone on a deserted island. One day in near despair, he opened his Bible at random. It opened to Psalm 107. What he read gave him the courage to persevere until his rescue in 1908.

They who sailed the sea in ships,
trading on the deep waters,
These saw the works of the LORD
and his wonders in the abyss.

His command raised up a storm wind
which tossed its waves on high.
They mounted up to heaven;
they sank to the depths;
their hearts melted away in their plight.

They cried to the LORD in their distress;
from their straits he rescued them.
He hushed the storm to a gentle breeze,
and the billows of the sea were stilled;

They rejoiced that they were calmed,
and he brought them to their desired haven.
Let them give thanks to the LORD
for his kindness
and his wondrous deeds to the children of men.
(23–26, 28–31)

Jesus "said to the sea, 'Quiet! Be still!' The wind ceased and there was great calm." *Mark 4:39*

Speak to Jesus about some storm in your life, and ask him to calm it.

Lord, your kindness towers to the heavens.

In 1939 Hitler's armies were poised to attack. England's future looked dark. On Christmas Day, King George VI addressed his people and counseled trust in God. He ended by quoting from a poem by Minnie Louise Haskins: "I said to the man / who stood at the gate of the year: / Give me a light / that I may tread safely into the unknown!' / And he replied: 'Go out into the darkness / and put your hand into the hand of God. / That shall be to you better than light / and safer than a known way.' " The psalmist expresses this same childlike faith in God in Psalm 108.

My heart is steadfast, O God;
my heart is steadfast;
I will sing and chant praise.
Awake, O my soul; awake, lyre and harp;
I will wake the dawn.
I will give thanks to you among the peoples,
O LORD;
I will chant your praise among the nations,
For your kindness towers to the heavens,
and your faithfulness to the skies.

Be exalted above the heavens, O God;
over all the earth be your glory! (2–6)

Paul writes, "We know that all things work for good for those who love God." *Romans 8:28*

Recall a time when your trust in God was pushed almost to the limit. Speak to Jesus about his own childlike trust in his Father and in other people.

Day four   Psalm 109

Save me, O Lord, in your kindness.

Marine Sergeant Jimmy Lopez was held hostage 444 days by Iranian terrorists. In an article entitled "How to Wait through a Long Darkness," Jimmy's mother tells how the Lopez family coped with the ordeal: "We put our trust in God." When things got unbearable, she said, "We talked with God the way Jesus did in the Garden of Gethsemane." Psalm 109 describes a man coping with a similar ordeal. He talks to God from the heart, as Jesus did in the Garden of Gethsemane.

O God, my Lord,
deal kindly with me for your name's sake;
in your generous kindness rescue me;
For I am wretched and poor,
and my heart is pierced within me.

Help me, O LORD, my God;
save me, in your kindness,
And let them know that this is your hand,
that you, O LORD, have done this.

I will speak my thanks earnestly to the LORD,
and in the midst of the throng I will praise him,
For he stood at the right hand of the poor man,
to save him from those
who would condemn him.   (21–22, 26–27, 30–31)

Jesus prayed in the garden: "Abba, Father, all things are possible to you. Take this cup away from me, but not what I will but what you will." *Mark 14:36*

Recall some ordeal you went through. Speak to Jesus about the purpose of such ordeals.

You are a priest for ever, in the line of Melchizedek.

The coronation of a new king in Israel was the occasion for a great religious celebration. For in light of God's promise to David, it brought the nation a step closer to the promised "King of Kings," the Messiah. This explains why Psalm 110 played such an important role in the coronation celebration.

*T**he* Lord *said to my Lord:*
"Sit at my right hand
till I make your enemies your footstool."

The scepter of your power
the Lord *will stretch forth from Zion:*
"Rule in the midst of your enemies.

"Yours is princely power in the day
of your birth, in holy splendor;
before the daystar, like the dew,
I have begotten you."

The Lord *has sworn, and he will not repent:*
"You are a priest forever,
according to the order of Melchizedek."   (1–4)

Jesus cites Psalm 110 (in which David calls the Messiah his Lord) to prove that the Messiah is far more than a mere "son of David."   (Matthew 22:41–45)   New Testament writers interpreted Psalm 110 as referring ultimately to Jesus. (Hebrews 1:13, 8:1)

Reread Psalm 110 slowly, pausing after each verse to speak to Jesus about what is said of him.

Day six

How great are the works of the Lord!

A poetic feature of some psalms (lost in translation) is "acrostic" composition. That is, each line starts with one of the twenty-two letters of the Hebrew alphabet. Thus, line one starts with *aleph* (A), line two with *beth* (B), and so on. Psalm 111 is composed like this. Other acrostic psalms include 25, 33, 44, 112, 119 (each verse). Psalm 111 ends with the "first principle" of biblical wisdom: "The fear of the Lord is the beginning of wisdom." *Fear* here means "profound reverence and awe," not panic or fright. *Wisdom* means "practical knowledge": knowing how to live in a way that will result in peace with one's self and with one's neighbor.

> *he works of his hands are faithful and just;*
> *sure are all his precepts,*
> *Reliable forever and ever,*
> *wrought in truth and equity.*
>
> *He has sent deliverance to his people;*
> *he has ratified his covenant forever;*
> *holy and awesome is his name.*
>
> *The fear of the Lord*
> *is the beginning of wisdom;*
> *prudent are all who live by it.*
> *His praise endures forever.* (7–10)

"If any of you lacks wisdom, he should ask God . . . and he will be given it." *James 1:5*

Speak to Jesus about anything that disturbs your inner contentment or social harmony.

The heart of the just man is secure, trusting in the Lord.

The Sea of Galilee is alive with fish; the Dead Sea hasn't seen a fish in centuries. Both seas are fed by the mountain streams. Why, then, is the one sea alive and fresh while the other is dead and salty? It's because the Sea of Galilee gives up as much water as it receives, letting it flow into the Jordan River. The Dead Sea keeps what it receives, losing only what the sun takes away from it by evaporation. The two seas are like the two kinds of people in the world: the givers and the keepers. The givers are alive and enjoy life. The keepers are dead and don't enjoy life. Psalm 112 talks about the givers.

Happy the man who fears the LORD,
who greatly delights in his commands.
His posterity shall be mighty upon the earth;
the upright generation shall be blessed.

An evil report he shall not fear;
his heart is firm, trusting in the LORD.
His heart is steadfast; he shall not fear
till he looks down upon his foes.

Lavishly he gives to the poor;
his generosity shall endure forever;
his horn shall be exalted in glory. (1-2, 7-9)

Jesus promised that God will give to us with the same generosity that we give to others. (Luke 6:38)

Recall a moment of generosity in your life. Speak to Jesus about why he could give so generously.

For reflection or discussion

INTRODUCTION In what sense are the psalms like windows? Explain how the psalms can be used as windows into the mind and heart of Jesus.

WEEK 15

1 Worship

Explain: "The test of worship is how far it makes us *more sensitive* to the 'beyond in our midst,' to the Christ in the hungry, the naked, the homeless, and the prisoner." *John Robinson*

Recall one of the most meaningful worship services you ever attended. What made it so?

What part of your Sunday worship do you find most meaningful? Least meaningful? Explain.

2 Trials

Explain: "Who never ate his bread in sorrow, / Who never spent the darksome hours / Weeping and watching for the morrow, / He knows you not, you heavenly Powers." *Goethe*

Recall a difficult trial that you once faced.

What are some useful purposes that trials serve in the lives of people?

WEEK 16

1 Worry

Explain: "Today is the tomorrow you worried about yesterday." *Anonymous*

What are several worries you have right now?

Why do you find it hard to follow this advice of Scripture: "Cast all your worries upon God because he cares for you"? *1 Peter 5:7*

2 Generosity

Explain: "The fragrance always remains in the hand that gives the rose." *Heda Bejar*

Recall a time when you were more generous than usual. What moved you to be so generous?

What keeps you from being more generous with yourself, your time, your resources?

Problem Psalms

9 *O God . . .*
Let them vanish like water. . . .
Let them dissolve
like a melting snail.

Psalm 58:7–9

A tourist pointed to an old wagon in a deserted western mining town and said, "Look at that wreck. Can you believe people used to ride in fool things like that!"

It is a mistake to judge the past by modern standards. One area where we tend to do this is in the psalms. For example, we criticize certain psalms for their self-righteous tone. Take Psalm 17:3, for example. There the psalmist says to God, "Though you try me with fire, you shall find no malice in me."

To the modern ear, this sounds self-righteous. But it didn't sound that way to the ancient Hebrews. It was just the way they expressed themselves. Thus the psalmist speaks to God in the same black-and-white way about his sinfulness: "My sin is before me always. . . . Cast me not out from your presence." *Psalm 51:5, 13*

Modern Christians also criticize certain psalms for their vengeful tone. A case in point is Psalm 58:7: "Oh God, smash their teeth in their mouths." When we read a line like this, we must keep in mind that the psalms were written at a time when Israel had no clear idea of life after death. The concept of reward and punishment in an afterlife did not emerge fully until the second century B.C., and only then in vague terms. Thus the psalmist assumed that God would punish the wicked and reward the good in *this* life. Seen in this light, the psalmist's prayer for vengeance was really a prayer for justice.

We must remember, too, that Israel's early ideas of God were primitive. Only with the passage of time and more revelation, especially through the prophets, did their ideas of God develop and mature.

Although the Book of Psalms was edited after Israel's concept of God had passed beyond some of the earlier ideas expressed in the psalms, the editor included them anyway. There is an honesty here that is appealing. By including these psalms, the editor provided a yardstick that enables us to measure how Israel's idea of God evolved and matured over the years.

Day one   Psalm 113

Blessed be the name of the Lord for ever.

Psalms 113–118 are known as the *Hallel*. This word is derived from the Hebrew word *Hallelujah*, which means "Praise the Lord." In modern times, as in the time of Jesus, these psalms are sung at major Jewish festivals. For example, the Passover meal begins with the first half of the Hallel (Psalms 113–114) and ends with the second half (Psalms 115–118).

raise, you servants of the Lord,
praise the name of the Lord.
Blessed be the name of the Lord
both now and forever.

From the rising to the setting of the sun
is the name of the Lord to be praised.
High above all nations is the Lord,
above the heavens is his glory.

Who is like the Lord, our God,
who is enthroned on high
and looks upon the heavens
and the earth below?
He raises up the lowly from the dust;
from the dunghill he lifts up the poor.   (1–7)

Jesus and the disciples began the Last Supper with this psalm. They ended it by singing the final half of the Hallel. Thus Mark concludes his narrative of the Last Supper, saying, "Then, after singing a hymn, they went out to the Mount of Olives." *Mark 14:26*

Imagine you are present as Jesus and the Apostles sing Psalm 113 at the start of the Last Supper. Speak to Jesus about its appropriateness.

Day two   Psalm **114**

Alleluia.

Three moments stand out in the history of the Israel-ites: the parting of the Red Sea, which allowed them to flee from Egypt; the quaking of Mount Sinai, which signaled God's presence on the mountain when he covenanted with them; and the halting of the Jordan River, which provided a path for them to enter the Promised Land. Psalm 114 celebrates these three memorable moments: "The sea be-held and fled; Jordan turned back. The mountains skipped like rams."

When Israel came forth from Egypt,
the house of Jacob
from a people of alien tongue,
Judah became his sanctuary,
Israel his domain.

The sea beheld and fled;
Jordan turned back.
The mountains skipped like rams,
the hills like the lambs of the flock.

Why is it, O sea, that you flee?
O Jordan, that you turn back?
You mountains, that you skip like rams?
You hills, like the lambs of the flock?   (1–6)

A sea, a mountain, and a river also figured in some memorable moments in Jesus' life. He calmed the Sea of Galilee, was baptized in the Jordan, and was transfigured on Mount Tabor.

Recall three memorable moments in your life, and speak to Jesus about them.

Day three

The house of Israel trusts in the Lord.

"The carpenter cuts down cedars. . . . With a part of their wood he warms himself, or makes a fire for baking bread; but with another part he makes a god which he adores, an idol which he worships . . . a thing that cannot save itself when the flame consumes it; yet he does not say, 'Is not this thing in my right hand a fraud?' " *Isaiah 44:14–15, 20* In passages like this, the prophets ridiculed the practice of idolatry. In similar passages, the psalmist ridiculed it also. For example, Psalm 115 compares the God of Israel to pagan idols.

> *Our God is in heaven;*
>   *whatever he wills, he does.*
>   *Their idols are silver and gold,*
>   *the handiwork of men.*
>
> *They have mouths but speak not;*
>   *they have eyes but see not;*
> *They have ears but hear not;*
>   *they have noses but smell not;*
>
> *They have hands but feel not;*
>   *they have feet but walk not.*
> *Their makers shall be like them,*
>   *everyone that trusts in them.* (3–7, 8)

Paul writes: "Put to death, then, the parts of you that are earthly: immorality, impurity, passions, evil desire, and the greed that is idolatry." *Colossians 3:5*

What are some of the idols in your life? Speak to God about them.

I will walk in the presence of the Lord, in the land of the living.

Someone said that Psalm 116 begins like a love letter: "I love you, Lord." It also continues like a love letter, written by someone who has just recovered from a serious physical or mental illness.

*love the LORD because he has heard
my voice in supplication,
Because he has inclined his ear to me
the day I called.*

*The cords of death encompassed me;
the snares of the nether world seized upon me;
I fell into distress and sorrow,
And I called upon the name of the LORD,
"O LORD, save my life!"*

*Gracious is the LORD and just;
yes, our God is merciful.
The LORD keeps the little ones;
I was brought low, and he saved me.*

*For he has freed my soul from death,
my eyes from tears, my feet from stumbling.
I shall walk before the LORD
in the lands of the living.*   (1–6, 8–9)

A leper came to Jesus for healing. Jesus said to him, " 'Be made clean.' The leprosy left him immediately, and he was made clean." *Mark 1:41–42*

Recall a grave illness you or a family member had. Talk to God about its effect on you, spiritually.

Go out to all the world, and tell the Good News.

If you're a trivia buff, you know that Psalm 117 is the shortest of all the psalms (two verses). But its message makes up for its brevity. It testifies to the "marching orders" God gave his people. He told them to "go out to all the world, and tell the Good News." "As I see it," wrote Martin Luther, "the whole book of the Acts was written because of this psalm." For the Acts of the Apostles is nothing more than the story of God's people responding to God's commission to invite all the nations to praise and glorify God.

*P**raise the LORD, all you nations;*
glorify him, all you peoples!
    For steadfast is his kindness toward us,
and the fidelity of the LORD endures forever.   (1–2)

Referring to the nations of the world, Paul said to the Romans: "How can they call on him in whom they have not believed? And how can they believe in him of whom they have not heard? And how can they hear without someone to preach? . . . As it is written, 'How beautiful are the feet of those who bring [the] good news!' "   *Romans 10:14–15*

What are you doing about your commission to be a messenger of the Good News? Speak to Jesus about your Christian commission, and ask him how you can best carry it out.

This is the day the Lord has made;
let us rejoice and be glad.

The Last Supper began with the singing of the first half of the Hallel (Psalms 113–114) and ended with the singing of the second half (Psalms 115–118). How prophetic Psalm 118 must have seemed to Jesus as he sang it at that moment.

Give thanks to the LORD, for he is good,
*   for his mercy endures forever.*
*   Let the house of Israel say,*
*   "His mercy endures forever."*

"The right hand of the LORD
*   has struck with power:*
*   the right hand of the LORD is exalted."*
I shall not die, but live,
*   and declare the works of the LORD.*

The stone which the builders rejected
*   has become the cornerstone.*
By the LORD has this been done;
*   it is wonderful in our eyes.*   (1–2, 15–16, 17, 22–23)

Peter said: "Jesus is 'the stone rejected by you, the builders, which has become the cornerstone.' There is no salvation through anyone else, nor is there any other name under heaven given to the human race by which we are to be saved."   *Acts 4:11–12*

Enter the mind of Jesus as he walks along under the stars toward Gethsemane, meditating on Psalm 118. Speak to him about his thoughts.

Lord. teach me your decrees.

The Sinai covenant transformed Israel from a ragtag band of fugitive slaves to God's chosen people. An important part of the Sinai covenant was the Ten Commandments. They were God's guidelines for freeing his people from selfishness and setting them on the road to love and service. Psalm 119 sums up Israel's feelings toward the Ten Commandments.

*How shall a young man
be faultless in his way?
    By keeping to your words.*

*With all my heart I seek you;
    let me not stray from your commands.*

*Within my heart I treasure your promise,
    that I may not sin against you.*

*Blessed are you, O LORD;
    teach me your statutes.*

*With my lips I declare
    all the ordinances of your mouth.*

*In the way of your decrees I rejoice,
    as much as in all riches.*   (9-14)

John writes: "The love of God is this, that we keep his commandments. And his commandments are not burdensome."   *1 John 5:3*

Do you rejoice in God's commandments "as much as in all riches"? Speak to Jesus about how he looked upon the commandments his Father gave Israel.

Woe is me that I sojourn in Meshech.

Psalm 120 begins a series of fifteen "pilgrim psalms," or "psalms of ascent." The series concludes with Psalm 134. Scholars say these psalms were sung by Jews living far distant from Jerusalem, as they "ascended" on foot to the city (2,300 feet above sea level) to celebrate major religious festivals. Psalm 120 decries the alien neighbors among whom many of these pilgrim Jews had to live and sojourn. The aliens were not peace–loving people. They were barbarians given to violence and war. This situation was a constant source of stress; often it was also a source of major distress. Psalm 120 must be read against this background.

*I*n my distress I called to the L̲ord̲.
　O L̲ord̲, deliver me from lying lip,
from treacherous tongue.
Woe is me that I sojourn in Meshech,
　that I dwell amid the tents of Kedar!

All too long have I dwelt
　with those who hate peace.
When I speak of peace,
　they are ready for war.   (1, 2, 5–7)

Paul writes: "The fruit of the Spirit is love, joy, peace, patience, kindness, generosity, faithfulness, gentleness, self–control." *Galatians 5:22–23*

How peaceful, kind, and gentle are you in your dealings with others? Speak to Jesus about how he remained so peaceful, kind, and gentle.

Our help is from the Lord who made heaven and earth.

Astronaut James Irwin said he was taken aback by the mountains on the moon: "They were not gray or brown. . . . They were golden. . . . Running through my reflections were the words of Psalm 121."

I lift up my eyes toward the mountains;
whence shall help come to me?
My help is from the LORD,
who made heaven and earth.

May he not suffer your foot to slip;
may he slumber not who guards you:
Indeed he neither slumbers nor sleeps,
the guardian of Israel.

The LORD is your guardian;
the LORD is your shade;
he is beside you at your right hand.
The sun shall not harm you by day,
nor the moon by night.

The LORD will guard you from all evil;
he will guard your life.
The LORD will guard your coming
and your going,
both now and forever.   (1–8)

"Approach the throne of grace to receive mercy and to find grace for timely help."   *Hebrews 4:16*

How confidently do you "approach the throne of grace" for "timely help"? Speak to Jesus about this.

Day three   Psalm 122

I rejoiced when I heard them say:
let us go to the house of the Lord.

Paul VI was the first pope to visit Jerusalem during his reign in office. The first thing he did when he set foot inside Saint Stephen's Gate was to kneel and recite Psalm 122.

*I rejoiced because they said to me,
"We will go up to the house of the Lord."
And now we have set foot
within your gates, O Jerusalem—*

*Jerusalem, built as a city
with compact unity.
To it the tribes go up,
the tribes of the Lord,*

*According to the decree for Israel,
to give thanks to the name of the Lord.
In it are set up judgment seats,
seats for the house of David.*

*Because of my relatives and friends
I will say, "Peace be within you!"
Because of the house of the Lord, our God,
I will pray for your good.* (1–5, 8–9)

Jesus loved Jerusalem, saying, "Jerusalem . . . how many times I yearned to gather your children together as a hen gathers her brood under her wings, but you were unwilling!" *Luke 13:34*

Speak to Jesus about why people still resist being gathered under his spiritual wings.

Day four   Psalm 123

Have mercy on us, Lord, have mercy.

Father Paul Belliveau's parish is a refugee camp in
Honduras. Ten thousand Salvadoran men, women, and
children are held prisoner there. Describing a scene in the
camp, Father Paul writes: "I saw many women in the chapel
praying. I entered and sat down. About eighty women were
saying the Stations of the Cross. Every station identified the
suffering of Jesus with the refugees. They told me they
called their group 'Mothers who have lost children due to
violence in El Salvador.' " Imagine one of these mothers
kneeling alone one night in the chapel, praying to God in
the words of Psalm 123.

> *To you I lift up my eyes*
> *who are enthroned in heaven.*
> *Behold, as the eyes of servants*
> *are on the hands of their masters,*
>
> *As the eyes of a maid*
> *are on the hands of her mistress,*
> *So are our eyes on the Lord, our God,*
> *till he have pity on us.*   (1–2)

Standing beneath the cross of Jesus were Mary and
John. "When Jesus saw his mother and the disciple there
whom he loved, he said to his mother, 'Woman, behold,
your son.' Then he said to the disciple, 'Behold, your mother.'
And from that hour the disciple took her into his home."
John 19:26–27

How sensitive are you to people's pain? Speak to Jesus
about his sensitivity to people's suffering.

Our help is in the name of the Lord.

An enormous Assyrian army arrived at the walled city of Jerusalem and prepared to attack it in the morning. Inside the city, the Jewish citizens were terrified. That night a deadly plague struck the Assyrian camp, decimating the army and forcing it to return home.   (2 Kings 19:35–36, Sirach 48:21)

*Had not the L*ORD *been with us,*
let Israel say,
*had not the L*ORD *been with us—*
When men rose up against us,
then would they have swallowed us alive.

When their fury was inflamed against us,
then would the waters have overwhelmed us;
The torrent would have swept over us;
over us then would have swept
the raging waters.
*Blessed be the L*ORD*, who did not leave us*
a prey to their teeth.

We were rescued like a bird
from the fowlers' snare;
Broken was the snare,
and we were freed.
*Our help is in the name of the L*ORD*,*
who made heaven and earth.   (1–8)

Jesus experienced his Father's help often. For example, he experienced it in Nazareth when an angry mob tried to hurl him over a cliff.   (Luke 4:28–30)

Recall a time when you experienced God's help in a special way. Speak to the Father about it.

They who trust in the Lord are like Mount Zion.

Imagine you live in Jesus' day. You are in a large group of people from tiny hamlets in Galilee. You are traveling to Jerusalem to celebrate the Passover. Suddenly the holy city comes into full view. As it gleams brightly in the morning sun, you no longer see mountains surrounding it. You see only the loving arms of God embracing it. Sitting down on the hillside, amid the wild flowers growing there, you and the rest of the pilgrims look toward Jerusalem and sing.

*They who trust in the L*ORD
are like Mount Zion,
which is immovable; which forever stands.

Mountains are round about Jerusalem;
*so the L*ORD *is round about his people,*
both now and forever.

*Do good, O L*ORD, *to the good*
and to the upright of heart.
Peace be upon Israel!   (1–2, 4, 5)

Jesus said, "Notice how the flowers grow. They do not toil or spin. But I tell you, not even Solomon in all his splendor was dressed like one of them. If God so clothes the grass in the field . . . will he not much more provide for you . . . ? Do not worry anymore."   *Luke 12:27–29*

Speak to God about why you sometimes find it hard to trust in his loving care.

Day seven   Psalm 126

The Lord has done marvels for us.

The crowd cheered wildly as a plane filled with American POWs from Vietnam hit the runway. A similar cheer burst forth from the POWs on the plane as it taxied to a stop. The joy that filled their hearts was the same joy that filled the hearts of Jewish POWs as they returned from Babylon in 538 B.C.

When the LORD
brought back the captives of Zion,
we were like men dreaming.
Then our mouth was filled with laughter,
and our tongue with rejoicing.

Then they said among the nations,
"The LORD has done great things for them."
The LORD has done great things for us;
we are glad indeed.

Restore our fortunes, O LORD,
like the torrents in the southern desert.
Those that sow in tears
shall reap rejoicing.

Although they go forth weeping,
carrying the seed to be sown,
They shall come back rejoicing,
carrying their sheaves.   (1-6)

Jesus said, "He has sent me . . . to let the oppressed go free." *Luke 4:18*

Speak to Jesus about the joy that fills your heart at his freeing you from spiritual captivity.

For reflection or discussion

INTRODUCTION   What are some things we should keep in mind in explaining the self-righteous or vengeful tone of certain psalms?

WEEK 17
1   Memory
Explain: "God gives us memory so that we may have roses in December."   *James Matthew Barrie*

Recall two of the most memorable moments in your life.

To what extent do you agree that "we are what we remember"?

2   Commandments
Explain: "We can't break the Ten Commandments; we can only break ourselves against them."   *Cecil B. DeMille*

Recall a time when you kept a commandment at great personal effort or personal sacrifice.

Why do you think the Ten Commandments are so blatantly pushed aside in modern society?

WEEK 18
1   God's loving care
Explain: "When God shuts a door, he opens a window."   *John Ruskin*

Recall a time when God shut a door in your life, but opened a window in its place.

How do you reconcile God's loving care with pain and suffering?

2   Prayer of petition
Explain: "Prayer is one of the ways that God chose to share his infinite power with us."   *Blaise Pascal*

Recall the most dramatic answer to a prayer that you ever received.

Why do/don't you think it is appropriate to pray to God for practical things like "good weather"?

Pilgrim Psalms

10

How happy are those . . .
who are eager to make
the pilgrimage to Mount Zion.

Psalm 84:5 (TEV)

Sidewalks did not exist in Jesus' time. There were just footpaths, worn smooth by thousands of feet passing over them. These footpaths began to teem with people at the approach of the three major Jewish holidays: Passover, Pentecost, and Tabernacles. People streamed out of small hamlets to join larger groups for the long pilgrimage to the Temple in Jerusalem.

One reason people joined larger groups for the journey was to protect themselves from bands of roving outlaws. (Luke 2:44) Recall the solitary traveler in the parable of the good Samaritan who was attacked by roving outlaws.

Another reason for walking in larger groups was for company and for entertainment. To make the hours pass more quickly, pilgrims sang psalms. They could be heard for miles around, as their voices echoed from hillsides and across fields.

A special medley of psalms was developed for the journey. For example, there were special psalms to be sung at the start of the pilgrimage, during the pilgrimage, and when the Temple first came into view. There were also psalms to be sung as the people approached the gates of the walled city and immediately as they entered the city gates. Thus, for example, Psalm 122:1–2 reads:

I rejoiced because they said to me,
  "We will go up to the house of the LORD."
And now we have set foot
  within your gates, O Jerusalem.

Psalms 120–134 each contain introductory notes saying "A song of ascents." Some scholars think these fifteen psalms were among those that were sung by the people on their pilgrimage to Jerusalem. We can imagine the excitement with which Jesus sang these "pilgrim psalms" on his first trip to Jerusalem at the age of twelve.

The distance from Nazareth to Jerusalem was about sixty-five miles. The trip would have taken several days to make on foot.

Day one 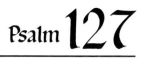 Psalm 127

The Lord will build a house for us and guard our city.

The Constitutional Convention was deadlocked in Philadelphia in 1787. The thirteen colonies could not agree on a form of central government. It was at this point that eighty-one-year-old Benjamin Franklin rose to his feet. Quoting the Book of Psalms, he said, "Unless the Lord build the house, they labor in vain who build it." Then he moved that the delegates begin the next day's meeting with prayer. The motion was carried. The deadlock was resolved, and a great new nation was born. To this day, Congress follows the example of the first Constitutional Convention and begins each session by praying for God's help and guidance.

Unless the Lord build the house,
they labor in vain who build it.
Unless the Lord guard the city,
in vain does the guard keep vigil.

It is vain for you to rise early,
or put off your rest,
You that eat hard-earned bread,
for he gives to his beloved in sleep. (1-2)

Jesus said, "What father among you would hand his son a snake when he asks for a fish? . . . If you then, who are wicked, know how to give good gifts to your children, how much more will the Father in heaven give the holy Spirit to those who ask him?" *Luke 11:11, 13*

Recall a time when God answered your prayer for guidance in some matter. Speak to God about this.

Day two   Psalm 128

See how the Lord blesses those who fear him.

From the day a dove brought an olive twig back to Noah after the flood, the olive tree has been a symbol of hope. No tree was more prized in Israel. People used olive oil to cook their food, heal their sick, and light their lamps. Small wonder the psalmist chose to compare children to tiny "olive plants" that would soon grow into fruitful trees. Addressing fathers, the psalmist says:

Happy are you who fear the LORD,
who walk in his ways!
For you shall eat the fruit of your handiwork;
happy shall you be, and favored.

Your wife shall be like a fruitful vine
in the recesses of your home;
Your children like olive plants
around your table.

Behold, thus is the man blessed
who fears the LORD.
The LORD bless you from Zion:
may you see the prosperity of Jerusalem
all the days of your life.   (1–5)

"Let the children come to me . . . for the kingdom of God belongs to such as these. Amen, I say to you, whoever does not accept the kingdom of God like a child will not enter it." *Mark 10:14–15*

Speak to Jesus about what it means to accept the kingdom of God like a child.

Day three

Psalm 129

The Lord has set us free.

Many Israelites were born in exile in Babylon and had known oppression from their youth. They had worked as slaves, and some had scars on their backs to show it. Then came the great day when King Cyrus of Persia conquered Babylon and allowed the Israelites to return home after fifty years of exile. They left Babylon, asking God to manifest his justice; for in hating them, Babylon had hated God.

Much have they oppressed me from my youth,
let Israel say,
Much have they oppressed me from my youth;
yet they have not prevailed against me.

Upon my back the plowers plowed;
long did they make their furrows
But the just LORD has severed
the cords of the wicked.

May all be put to shame and fall back
that hate Zion.
May they be like grass on the housetops,
which withers before it is plucked;
With which the reaper fills not his hand,
nor the gatherer of sheaves his arms. (1-7)

Jesus said, "Some seed fell on rocky ground, and when it grew, it withered for lack of moisture. Some seed fell among thorns, and the thorns grew with it and choked it." *Luke 8:6–7*

Speak to Jesus about your concern for other people, especially the displaced and the oppressed.

Day four Psalm 130

Out of the depths, I cry to you, Lord.

Tchaikovsky's *1812 Overture* celebrates Russia's victory over Napoleon's invading armies. It portrays this by having the Russian hymn gradually drown out the French national anthem. Something like this happens in Psalm 130. The psalmist's confidence in God's mercy gradually drowns out his fear of God's punishment.

Out of the depths I cry to you, O LORD.
LORD, hear my voice!
Let your ears be attentive
to my voice in supplication:

If you, O LORD, mark iniquities,
LORD, who can stand?
But with you is forgiveness,
that you may be revered.

I trust in the LORD;
my soul trusts in his word.
My soul waits for the LORD
more than sentinels wait for the dawn.

More than sentinels wait for the dawn,
let Israel wait for the LORD,
For with the LORD is kindness
and with him is plenteous redemption;
And he will redeem Israel
from all their iniquities.　(1-8)

Jesus said to the sinful woman, "Your sins are forgiven. . . . Your faith has saved you." *Luke 7:48, 50*

Speak to Jesus about his death on the cross, by which he redeemed us from our sins.

In you, Lord, I have found my peace.

Someone compared this tiny psalm to the ringing of a church bell in a peaceful valley just as the setting sun casts a soft golden glow on everything below. It is the kind of prayer that would be found on the lips of the *ani* ("poor people") of Jesus' time. They were people who were economically and politically helpless. In such a situation, these people became completely detached from material things and totally attached to God.

> *O Lord, my heart is not proud,*
> *nor are my eyes haughty;*
> *I busy not myself with great things,*
> *nor with things too sublime for me.*
>
> *Nay rather, I have stilled and quieted*
> *my soul like a weaned child.*
> *Like a weaned child on its mother's lap,*
> *[so is my soul within me.]*
>
> *O Israel, hope in the Lord,*
> *both now and forever.*   (1–3)

Jesus said, "Blessed are the poor in spirit, for theirs is the kingdom of heaven." *Matthew 5:3* Jesus had in mind those people who had come to realize they could not depend on material things for happiness. So they sought their happiness in God alone. God meant everything to them; materials things meant next to nothing. These humble people were truly blessed.

How "poor in spirit" are you? Speak to Jesus about his own poverty in spirit.

The Lord has chosen Zion for his dwelling.

God's pledge of an eternal kingship to David began a series of promises that pointed to a person called the Messiah. The word *Messiah* means "anointed one," or "king." The messianic promises reached their ultimate fulfillment in Jesus.

> *he* Lord *swore to David*
> *a firm promise from which*
> *he will not withdraw:*
> *"Your own offspring*
>   *I will set upon your throne;*
>
> *"If your sons keep my covenant*
>   *and the decrees which I shall teach them,*
> *Their sons, too, forever*
>   *shall sit upon your throne."*
>
> *For the* Lord *has chosen Zion;*
>   *he prefers her for his dwelling.*
> *"Zion is my resting place forever;*
>   *in her will I dwell, for I prefer her.*
>
> *"In her will I make a horn*
>   *to sprout forth for David;*
>   *I will place a lamp for my anointed.*
> *His enemies I will clothe with shame,*
>   *but upon him my crown shall shine."*   (11–14, 17–18)

Speaking about Jesus, the angel said to Mary, "The Lord God will give him the throne of David his father . . . and of his kingdom there will be no end." *Luke 1:32–33*

Speak to Jesus about his kingdom and the role he wants you to play in bringing it to completion.

How good it is
when brethren dwell together in harmony.

In *Instant Replay: The Green Bay Diary of Jerry Kramer,* Jerry describes how he felt after the Packers won their third straight championship: "We rushed to the locker room, laughing and shouting and absolutely floating. . . . I felt so proud, proud of myself and proud of my teammates and proud of my coaches. I felt like I was a part of something special. . . . It's the feeling of being together, completely together, a singleness of purpose, accomplishing something that a lot of people thought you couldn't accomplish. It sent a beautiful shiver up my back." It is this kind of feeling that Psalm 133 celebrates.

ehold, how good it is, and how pleasant,
where brethren dwell at one!
It is as when the precious ointment
upon the head
runs down over the beard, the beard of Aaron,
till it runs down upon the collar of his robe.

It is a dew like that of Hermon,
which comes down upon the mountains of Zion;
For there the Lord *has pronounced his blessing,*
life forever. (1-3)

Jesus prayed, "May all be one, as you, Father, are in me and I in you . . . that the world may believe that you sent me." *John 17:21*

Speak to Jesus about how you are contributing to unity in your family, your church, and your community.

Come, bless the Lord,
all you servants of the Lord.

A TV "news-magazine program" did a fascinating story on the night workers in stores and office buildings in our cities. They are the people who clean, maintain, and secure these buildings. They are the people who work behind the scenes to make these buildings function efficiently during the day. A similar group of people worked at similar jobs in the Jerusalem Temple.   (1 Chronicles 9:26-34)   They cleaned the Temple, maintained it, and kept it secure. Appropriately, the tiny psalm that concludes the series of "pilgrim psalms" takes the form of a blessing on these behind-the-scenes people.

> *ome, bless the LORD,*
> *all you servants of the LORD*
> *Who stand in the house of the LORD*
> *during the hours of night.*
>
> *Lift up your hands toward the sanctuary,*
> *and bless the LORD.*
> *May the LORD bless you from Zion,*
> *the maker of heaven and earth.*   (1-3)

The Gospel makes it clear that Jesus also did behind-the-scenes work at night. For example, Luke says that Jesus "departed to the mountain to pray, and he spent the night in prayer to God."   *Luke 6:12*

How generously do you give yourself to behind-the-scenes work for others, like members of your family, your church, or your community? Speak to Jesus about this aspect of your life.

Praise the Lord for he is good!

James H. Cone's book *God of the Oppressed* has a beautiful description of worship in the black community in slave days: "Through song, prayer, and sermon the community affirmed Jesus' presence and their willingness to make it through a troubled situation. Some would smile and others would cry. Another person, depending upon the Spirit's effect on him, would clap his hands and tap his feet. . . . All of these expressions were nothing but black people bearing witness to Jesus' presence among them. He was the divine power in their lives." Psalm 135 calls Israel to a similar worship.

Praise, you servants of the LORD
Who stand in the house of the LORD,
in the courts of the house of our God.

Praise the LORD, for the LORD is good;
sing praise to his name, which we love;
For the LORD has chosen Jacob for himself,
Israel for his own possession.

For I know that the LORD is great;
our LORD is greater than all gods.
All that the LORD wills he does
in heaven and on earth,
in the seas and in all the deeps.   (1–6)

"Where two or three are gathered together in my name, there am I in the midst of them."   *Matthew 18:20*

What does worship mean to you? Speak to Jesus about how it can begin to mean more to you.

His love is everlasting.

A massive army invaded Israel. The people prayed and fasted. As the Israelite soldiers neared the battle site, they began singing Psalm 136. At that moment a catastrophe struck the invaders and Israel was saved. (2 Chronicles 20:20–23)

> *ive thanks to the LORD, for he is good,*
>   *for his mercy endures forever;*
>   *Give thanks to the God of gods,*
>   *for his mercy endures forever;*
> *Give thanks to the Lord of lords,*
>   *for his mercy endures forever.*
>
> *Who led his people through the wilderness,*
>   *for his mercy endures forever;*
> *Who smote great kings,*
>   *for his mercy endures forever;*
> *And slew powerful kings,*
>   *for his mercy endures forever.*
>
> *And made their land a heritage,*
>   *for his mercy endures forever;*
> *The heritage of Israel his servant,*
>   *for his mercy endures forever;*
> *And freed us from our foes,*
>   *for his mercy endures forever.* (1–3, 16–18, 21–22, 24)

"If you have faith the size of a mustard seed, you would say to [this] mulberry tree, 'Be uprooted and planted in the sea,' and it would obey you." *Luke 17:6*

Speak to Jesus about your faith and your readiness to act on it in complete trust.

Day four   Psalm 137

Let my tongue be silenced,
if I ever forget you!

In *God of the Oppressed* James H. Cone asks how black slaves could keep going day after day. How could they keep hoping year after year? It was because they placed God ahead of themselves and remembered his love for them. It is against a similar background that the psalmist composed Psalm 137.

*B*y the streams of Babylon
we sat and wept
when we remembered Zion.
On the aspens of that land
we hung up our harps,

Though there our captors asked of us
the lyrics of our songs,
And our despoilers urged us to be joyous:
"Sing for us the songs of Zion!"

How could we sing a song of the LORD
in a foreign land?
If I forget you, Jerusalem,
may my right hand be forgotten!

May my tongue cleave to my palate
if I remember you not,
If I place not Jerusalem
ahead of my joy.   (1-6)

Jesus said, "Remain in me, as I remain in you."   John 15:4

Speak to Jesus about how your faith supports you in times of trial and difficulty.

Lord, I thank you
for your faithfulness and love.

A retreat master has read over five thousand "letters to God," written by teenagers on retreats. An unexpected discovery about these letters is that over 40 percent have gratitude to God as their main theme. This is also a main theme in the psalms.

I will give thanks to you, O LORD,
with all my heart,
[for you have heard the words of my mouth;]
in the presence of the angels
I will sing your praise;
I will worship at your holy temple
and give thanks to your name,

Because of your kindness and your truth;
for you have made great above all things
your name and your promise.
When I called, you answered me;
you built up strength within me.

All the kings of the earth
shall give thanks to you, O LORD,
when they hear the words of your mouth;
And they shall sing of the ways of the LORD:
"Great is the glory of the LORD." (1–5)

Jesus sent ten lepers to the authorities. On their way they were cured. Only one, however, returned "to give thanks to God." *Luke 17:18*

Speak to Jesus about how you show gratitude to God for his many gifts to you.

You have searched me and you know me, Lord.

During World War II, Eddie Rickenbacker and a crew of seven crashed into the Pacific. After a week it rained and the men were able to collect water to drink. On another occasion two fish leaped into their rubber raft. One of the things that kept them going throughout the twenty-one-day ordeal was a daily prayer session. One of the most popular prayers during these sessions was Psalm 139.

Where can I go from your spirit?
from your presence where can I flee?
If I go up to the heavens, you are there;
if I sink to the nether world,
you are present there.

If I take the wings of the dawn,
if I settle at the farthest limits of the sea,
Even there your hand shall guide me,
and your right hand hold me fast.

If I say, "Surely the darkness shall hide me,
and night shall be my light"—
For you darkness itself is not dark,
and night shines as the day. *(7–12)*

"Do not seek what you are to eat and . . . drink, and do not worry anymore. . . . Your Father knows that you need them. Instead, seek his kingdom, and these other things will be given you." *Luke 12:29–31*

How trusting are you in God's providence over you? Speak to Jesus about your answer.

Day seven  Psalm 140

Save us, O Lord, from evil men.

"Nobody's safe in the streets of Los Angeles anymore!" "Do something about these gangs!" Cries like these stirred Los Angeles authorities into action. A thousand-officer sweep of gang-infested areas was ordered. "We are going to take these terrorists off the street," Mayor Tom Bradley told the officers. "Police with shotguns," reported *USA Today*, "rousted suspected gang members, forcing them to kneel on the sidewalk with hands clasped behind their heads." When the sweep ended, 1,200 arrests were recorded. The psalmist cried out to God for similar action in Psalm 140.

*D*eliver me, O L*ORD*, from evil men;
preserve me from violent men,
From those who devise evil in their hearts.

Save me, O L*ORD*, from the hands
of the wicked;
by the wayside they have laid snares.

Hearken, O L*ORD*, to my voice
in supplication.
O God, my Lord, my strength and my salvation.

(2–3, 5, 6, 7–8)

Jesus said, "A man fell victim to robbers. . . . They stripped and beat him and went off leaving him half-dead." *Luke 10:30*

What are you doing about violence in the world? Is your voice being heard? Speak to Jesus about what he would do if he were living in today's world.

For reflection or discussion

<u>INTRODUCTION</u>   When did large numbers of pilgrims journey to Jerusalem? Why did they try to journey together in large groups? Which psalms developed out of these journeys, and what name is given to them? Read Luke 2:41–50. How does it reflect the size of the pilgrim groups and their spirit?

<u>WEEK 19</u>

1   Children
Explain: "You must ask children and birds how cherries and strawberries taste."   Goethe

Recall a pleasant childhood memory.

What do you think is lacking most in the lives of children today?

2   Community
Explain: "In prayer we should always unite ourselves to the community."   Jewish Talmud

Recall a community service you have performed in the past. Why did you do it?

Why do you think people are becoming more (or less) community–minded today?

<u>WEEK 20</u>

1   Work
Explain: "When it comes to work, the morning is wiser than the evening."   Russian proverb

What kind of work do you like most? Least?

What are some things that keep people from taking pride in their work the way they should?

2   Gratitude
Explain: "Gratitude is the heart's memory."   Anonymous

Call to mind three people, besides your parents, to whom you owe a great debt of gratitude. Explain.

What are three ways to express gratitude? Evaluate them in terms of effectiveness.

Timelessness
of the
Psalms

11 *Call upon me in time of distress;
I will rescue you,
and you shall glorify me.*

Psalm 50:15

Recently the news media carried a story entitled "Saved by a Psalm." It concerned a New Mexico woman, Spider Kathleen Baker-Gumprecht, who had a close call in a hot-air balloon. In the midst of her life-and-death ordeal, she discovered herself praying a psalm that she had memorized in childhood: "Call upon me in time of distress; I will rescue you, and you shall glorify me."   *Psalm 50:15*   She says: "Suddenly, I knew I wasn't alone. I felt calmed. Strength poured through me. Something urged me to work the burner . . . though this didn't seem to make sense. After all I was already spiraling upward."

Senseless or not, the idea worked. Fifteen minutes later, she was on the ground, safe and sound.

What happened to the woman balloonist that morning on a stretch of desert outside Albuquerque was something she would never forget. But what stood out more than anything else was the realization that a three-thousand-year-old prayer had helped save her life. It had put her in touch with a living, caring presence. And that presence calmed her, strengthened her, and guided her.

That morning the woman discovered what so many other Christians have discovered over the centuries: The psalms are timeless prayers. They are as meaningful and as relevant today as they were when David prayed them in the forest of Hereth, or when Francis sang them in the fields of Assisi, or when Ignatius meditated on them in the caves of Montserrat.

The woman concluded her story, saying that now when she is floating upward in her balloon, she doesn't feel she is getting farther from earth; she simply feels she is getting "closer to God."

Let my prayer come like incense before you.

Saint Francis of Assisi was born to a wealthy Italian family in 1182. As a teenager he was a playboy. At the age of twenty he joined the army, was captured, and spent a year in chains. After his release he turned his back on his family wealth and began to preach the Gospel on street corners. Young people flocked to him. At the age of twenty-seven he founded a religious order that thrives to this day. On October 3, 1226, at the age of forty-four, Francis died, praying Psalm 141.

> *O* LORD, *to you I call; hasten to me;*
> *hearken to my voice when I call upon you.*
> *Let my prayer come like incense before you;*
> *the lifting up of my hands,*
> *like the evening sacrifice.*
>
> *O* LORD, *set a watch before my mouth,*
> *a guard at the door of my lips.*
> *For toward you, O God, my Lord,*
> *my eyes are turned;*
> *in you I take refuge.* (1–3, 8)

A rich young man asked Jesus what he must do to gain eternal life. Jesus said, "Keep the commandments." When the young man said he was doing this, Jesus said to him, "If you wish to be perfect, go, sell what you have and give to [the] poor, and you will have treasure in heaven. Then come, follow me." *Matthew 19:17, 21*

Imagine you are the young man who approached Jesus. Speak to the Master about his words to you.

With a loud voice I cry to the Lord.

Paul Kordenbrock is a prisoner on Death Row in the Kentucky State Penitentiary. He underwent a remarkable conversion and has helped a number of other prisoners to find Christ. An appeal to have his case reviewed was turned down. Shortly afterward he wrote: "At times being a Christian seems easy. . . . You feel as if Christ would be well pleased with your life and how you are living for him. There are also times when nothing you think, do, or say feels right. . . . You catch yourself wondering if it is even possible to be a follower of Christ." Paul is the kind of person who finds it easy to relate to the feelings of the person described in Psalm 142.

With a loud voice I cry out to the Lord;
with a loud voice I beseech the Lord.
Before him I lay bare my distress.
There is no one who cares for my life.

I cry out to you, O Lord;
I say, "You are my refuge."
Attend to my cry,
for I am brought low indeed.
Lead me forth from prison,
that I may give thanks to your name.   (2, 3, 5–6, 7, 8)

Jesus said, "If anyone wishes to come after me, he must deny himself and take up his cross daily and follow me."   *Luke 9:23*

How do you handle times of darkness and trial in your life? Speak to Jesus about how he handled times of trial and discouragement in his life.

O Lord, hear my prayer.

"In my wanting, hoping, wishing to get off Death Row," wrote prisoner Paul Kordenbrock, "I strayed. . . . I let prayer become a habit, not the true desire-longing for God that he so graciously taught me." Psalm 143 is a "desire-longing for God."

O Lord, *hear my prayer;*
hearken to my pleading in your faithfulness;
in your justice answer me.
And enter not into judgment with your servant,
for before you no living man is just.

I remember the days of old;
I meditate on all your doings,
the works of your hands I ponder.
I stretch out my hands to you;
my soul thirsts for you like parched land.

Hasten to answer me, O Lord,
for my spirit fails me.
At dawn let me hear of your kindness,
for in you I trust.

Teach me to do your will,
for you are my God.
May your good spirit guide me
on level ground.   (1–2, 5–7, 8, 10)

Jesus said, "I do not seek my own will but the will of the one who sent me."   *John 5:30*

Speak to Jesus about prayer, and ask him to teach you to pray with "true desire-longing for God."

Day four

Blessed be the Lord, my Rock!

One afternoon Augustus Toplady of Blangdon, England, was walking across the countryside. Suddenly a storm blew up, and he took cover in the cleft of a huge rock. As lightning flashed and thunder clapped, he realized how safe he was inside the rock. Then a strange thought struck him. Jesus Christ is like this rock. He protects us from the storms of life. Slowly the words of a hymn were born in his mind: "Rock of Ages, cleft for me, / Let me hide myself in thee. . . . / While I draw this fleeting breath, / When my eyes shall close in death, . . . / Rock of Ages, cleft for me, / Let me hide myself in thee." Like the hymn "Rock of Ages," Psalm 144 contrasts "God the rock" with "man the passing shadow."

B lessed be the Lord, my rock;
My refuge and my fortress,
*   my stronghold, my deliverer,*
My shield, in whom I trust.

Lord, what is man, that you notice him;
*   the son of man, that you take thought of him?*
Man is like a breath;
*   his days, like a passing shadow.*   (1, 2, 3–4)

Paul compares Jesus to a rock.   (1 Corinthians 10:4)   Jesus not only shelters those who seek refuge in him but also gives drink to those who are thirsty (as the desert rock did for the Israelites).   (Exodus 17:6)

Speak to Jesus about why you turn (or don't turn) to him for protection during the storms of life and for drink during the droughts of life.

Day five   Psalm **145**

The Lord is kind and merciful.

"I once viewed God as the eye in the sky," said a student. "He was hiding behind a cloud, like a cop with his radar gun, ready to zap me when I got out of line. It was a real relief to hear Jesus say that he was more like a loving father, waiting to embrace me when I came home after a bad scene." Psalm 145 reflects the merciful, compassionate God that Jesus preached.

*T*he Lord *is gracious and merciful,*
slow to anger and of great kindness.
The Lord is good to all
and compassionate toward all his works.

The Lord is faithful in all his words
and holy in all his works.
The Lord lifts up all who are falling
and raises up all who are bowed down.

The Lord is just in all his ways
and holy in all his works.
The Lord is near to all who call upon him,
to all who call upon him in truth.   (8–9, 13–14, 17–18)

For eighteen years a woman "was bent over, completely incapable of standing erect. When Jesus saw her, he . . . laid his hands on her, and she at once stood up straight and glorified God."   *Luke 13:11–13*

What is your image of God? Is he one who "lifts up all who are falling and raises up all who are bowed down"? Speak to God about your image.

Day six   Psalm **146**

Praise the Lord, my soul!

Jesus read from Isaiah: "The Lord . . . has anointed me / to bring glad tidings to the poor. / He has sent me to proclaim liberty to captives / and recovery of sight to the blind, / to let the oppressed go free."   *Luke 4:18*   Jesus then told the people that he was the one of whom Isaiah spoke. What Psalm 146 attributes to God, Jesus attributed to himself.

*P*raise the LORD, O my soul;
   I will praise the LORD all my life;
   I will sing praise to my God while I live.

[The LORD] keeps faith forever,
   secures justice for the oppressed,
   gives food to the hungry.

The LORD sets captives free;
   the LORD gives sight to the blind.
The LORD raises up those
    that were bowed down;
   the LORD loves the just.

The LORD protects strangers;
   the fatherless and the widow he sustains,
   but the way of the wicked he thwarts.
The LORD shall reign forever;
   your God, O Zion, through all generations.   (1–2, 6–10)

Jesus gave food to the hungry and sight to the blind. He raised up those that were bowed down.

Speak to Jesus about the deeper meaning behind his words and actions.

Praise the Lord
who heals the brokenhearted.

Eleven-year-old Trevor Ferrell was shocked to see on TV how Philadelphia's street people scrounged for food and warmth. He began collecting blankets and food and making nightly trips into the city to distribute them. Contributions poured in. The city honored Trevor, citing his work as an example of "compassion and mercy that knows no age." The personal God of Psalm 147 gave us those qualities.

P raise the LORD, for he is good;
sing praise to our God, for he is gracious;
it is fitting to praise him.
The LORD rebuilds Jerusalem;
the dispersed of Israel he gathers.

He heals the brokenhearted
and binds up their wounds.
He tells the number of the stars;
he calls each by name.

Great is our LORD and mighty in power:
to his wisdom there is no limit.
The LORD sustains the lowly;
the wicked he casts to the ground.   (1-6)

"Whoever does not love a brother whom he has seen cannot love God whom he has not seen."   *1 John 4:20*

How might you better imitate the God of Psalm 147, a God who heals the brokenhearted and sustains the lowly? Speak to Jesus about your answer.

Day one Psalm 148

Let all praise the name of the Lord.

Saint Francis of Assisi's famous "Canticle of Brother Sun" praises God and all creation. Psalm 148 may have inspired that magnificent composition.

Praise the Lord from the heavens,
praise him in the heights;
Praise him, all you his angels,
praise him, all you his hosts.

Praise him, sun and moon;
praise him, all you shining stars.
Praise him, you highest heavens,
and you waters above the heavens.

You mountains and all you hills,
you fruit trees and all you cedars;
You wild beasts and all tame animals,
you creeping things and you winged fowl.

Let the kings of the earth and all peoples,
the princes and all the judges of the earth,
Young men too, and maidens,
old men and boys [praise him].

Praise the name of the Lord,
for his name alone is exalted;
His majesty is above earth and heaven.   (1–4, 9–13)

Filled with joy, Jesus said, "I give you praise, Father, Lord of heaven and earth."   *Luke 10:21*

What are some ways you can praise God? Speak to Jesus about these various ways.

The Lord takes delight in his people.

Antal Dorati, the former conductor of Washington's National Symphony Orchestra, was being interviewed. The subject turned to dance—ballet. Mr. Dorati said that he believed that dance in its finest form was an act of praise. "I imagine," he said, "that the first dance was a movement of adoration . . . the body simply moving to give thanks to the creator." The psalmist felt the same way about dance. Psalm 149 is one of several examples that illustrate this.

> *Sing to the LORD a new song*
> *of praise in the assembly of the faithful.*
> *Let Israel be glad in their maker,*
> *let the children of Zion rejoice in their king.*
>
> *Let them praise his name in the festive dance,*
> *let them sing praise to him*
> *with timbrel and harp.*
> *For the LORD loves his people,*
> *and he adorns the lowly with victory.*
>
> *Let the faithful exult in glory;*
> *let them sing for joy upon their couches;*
> *Let the high praises of God be in their throats.*
> *This is the glory of all his faithful. Alleluia.*   (1–6, 9)

Jesus said that when the prodigal son returned home, the boy's father (God, in the parable) called for a celebration. Soon the house was filled with the sound of "music and dancing." *Luke 15:25*

Speak to God about how you can begin to use ordinary things like dancing as acts of praise to him.

Let everything that breathes
praise the Lord!

Handel's *Hallelujah Chorus* excites audiences because it brings together a magnificent harmony of human voices and musical instruments. Violins, horns, and drums—every musical instrument human genius has devised—combine to praise God. The same is true of Psalm 150. Written as a finale to worship, it was sung, played, and danced. It can be read in twenty seconds but took closer to twenty minutes—or even two hours—to perform. A conductor coordinated the whole, signaling when each group was to come in.

raise the Lord in his sanctuary,
praise him in the firmament of his strength.
Praise him for his mighty deeds,
praise him for his sovereign majesty.

Praise him with the blast of the trumpet,
praise him with lyre and harp,
Praise him with timbrel and dance,
praise him with strings and pipe.

Praise him with sounding cymbals,
praise him with clanging cymbals.
Let everything that has breath
praise the Lord! Alleluia.   (1–6)

"You were once darkness, but now you are light in the Lord. Live as children of light . . . singing and playing to the Lord in your hearts." *Ephesians 5:8, 19*

As you conclude your meditation program on the psalms, talk to Jesus about how it has helped you.

For reflection or discussion

Take a few minutes to review the psalms in this book. Pick out two or three that speak to your heart, even though they were written for hearts 2,500 years ago. Why are the psalms timeless?

WEEK 21

1 Crosses

Explain: "Tears may flow in the night, but joy comes in the morning."   *Psalm 30:5 (TEV)*

Recall a cross in your life that eventually turned out to be a blessing in disguise.

What advice would you give to a person carrying a heavy cross?

2 Compassion

Explain: "Help row the other's boat across, and lo! thine own has reached the shore."   *Hindu proverb*

What person or group of persons does your heart go out to a great deal today? Why them?

What might you do to give expression to your compassion for this person or group?

WEEK 22

1 Music and dance

Explain: "Music is a strange bird singing the songs of another shore."   *J. G. Holland*

Recall a song from your youth that holds a special place in your heart. Why this song?

What are one or two religious songs that move you in a special way during worship services?

2 Review and evaluation

Explain: "Prayer enlarges the heart until it is capable of containing God's gift of himself."   *Mother Teresa*

What did you find most beneficial or meaningful about this meditation program?

Where might you go from here? What follow-up might be appropriate for you or this group?

Appendix A

Mood Reading

An excellent way to use *The Psalms for Today* is as mood reading. Simply keep it handy for those times when you want to read something that fits a certain mood or situation you are in. For example, read the following psalms when you are:

Longing for God

42	My soul is thirsting for the living God.
63	My soul is thirsting for you, O Lord my God.
84	Here God lives among his people.
143	O Lord, hear my prayer.

Worried

4	Lord, let your face shine on us.
13	All my hope, O Lord, is in your loving kindness.
23	The Lord is my shepherd, there is nothing I shall want.
27	The Lord is my light and my salvation.
56	I will walk in the presence of God, with the light of the living.
121	Our help is from the Lord who made heaven and earth.

Sick or suffering

22	My God, my God, why have you abandoned me?
38	Forsake me not, O Lord.
69	Turn to the Lord in your need, and you will live.
86	Listen, Lord, and answer me.
88	Let my prayer come before you, Lord.
109	Save me, O Lord, in your kindness.
123	Have mercy on us, Lord, have mercy.

Grateful

33   Cry out with joy in the Lord, you holy ones; sing a new song to him.

66   Let all the earth cry out to God with joy.

98   All the ends of the earth have seen the saving power of God.

116   I will walk in the presence of the Lord, in the land of the living.

Happy

96   The Lord comes to judge the earth.

148   Let all praise the name of the Lord.

149   The Lord takes delight in his people.

150   Let everything that breathes praise the Lord!

Needing God's help

3   Lord, rise up and save me.

7   Lord, my God, I take shelter in you.

107   Give thanks to the Lord, his love is everlasting.

124   Our help is in the name of the Lord.

Needing God's forgiveness

6   Rescue me because of your kindness.

32   Lord, forgive the wrong I have done.

51   Be merciful, O Lord, for we have sinned.

91   In you, my God, I place my trust.

103   The Lord is kind and merciful.

Needing to trust God

31   Into your hands, O Lord, I entrust my spirit.

36   You are the source of life, O Lord.

40   Lord, come to my aid!

62   Rest in God alone, my soul.

108   Lord, your kindness towers to the heavens.

125   They who trust in the Lord are like Mount Zion.

144   Blessed be the Lord, my Rock!

Appendix B

Psalm References

For readers who wish to know where the responsorial psalms used in this book occur in the liturgy (Catholic), the following references to the *Lectionary for Mass* will be helpful. The numbers following the psalm references are to page numbers in the lectionary.

1   *What Are the Psalms?*

Psalm 1, 154; Psalm 2, 379; Psalm 3, 447; Psalm 4, 110; Psalm 5, 539; Psalm 6 (not used in the liturgy); Psalm 7, 356; Psalm 8, 263; Psalm 9, 681; Psalm 10, 567; Psalm 11 (not used in the liturgy); Psalm 12, 475; Psalm 13, 704 (whole psalm reprinted); Psalm 14 (not used in the liturgy).

2   *Who Wrote the Psalms?*

Psalm 15, 191 (whole psalm reprinted); Psalm 16, 109; Psalm 17, 653; Psalm 18, 366; Psalm 19, 686; Psalm 20 ((not used in the liturgy); Psalm 21, 426; Psalm 22, 72; Psalm 23, 59; Psalm 24, 439; Psalm 25, 141; Psalm 26, 539 (three verses added); Psalm 27, 52; Psalm 28, 646.

3   *Themes of the Psalms*

Psalm 29, 44 (four lines added); Psalm 30, 98; Psalm 31, 840; Psalm 32, 171 (one verse omitted); Psalm 33, 303; Psalm 34, 63; Psalm 35 (not used in the liturgy); Psalm 36, 574; Psalm 37, 860; Psalm 38 (not used in the liturgy); Psalm 39 (not used in the liturgy); Psalm 40, 206; Psalm 41, 156; Psalm 42, 709.

4   *Poetry of the Psalms*

Psalm 43, 661; Psalm 44, 422; Psalm 45, 641; Psalm 46, 352; Psalm 47, 126; Psalm 48, 527; Psalm 49, 481; Psalm 50, 734; Psalm 51, 46; Psalm 52, 632 (four lines added); Psalm 53 (not used in the liturgy); Psalm 54, 636 (three lines added); Psalm 55, 1068 (nine lines omitted); Psalm 56, 654.

5 Imagery of the Psalms

Psalm 57, 402; Psalm 58 (not used in the liturgy); Psalm 59, 582 (three lines omitted); Psalm 60, 526; Psalm 61 (not used in the liturgy); Psalm 62, 159; Psalm 63, 494; Psalm 64 (not used in the liturgy); Psalm 65, 511; Psalm 66, 122; Psalm 67, 40; Psalm 68, 409 (two lines added); Psalm 69, 560; Psalm 70 (not used in the liturgy).

6 The Psalms and God

Psalm 71, 146; Psalm 72, 43; Psalm 73 (not used in the liturgy); Psalm 74, 535 (two verses omitted); Psalm 75 (not used in the liturgy); Psalm 76 (not used in the liturgy); Psalm 77, 596; Psalm 78, 198; Psalm 79, 531 (three lines omitted); Psalm 80, 230 (one line omitted); Psalm 81, 464; Psalm 82, 721; Psalm 83 (not used in the liturgy); Psalm 84, 747.

7 The Psalms and the New Testament

Psalm 85, 570; Psalm 86, 449; Psalm 87, 666; Psalm 88, 667; Psalm 89, 991; Psalm 90, 497; Psalm 91, 496; Psalm 92, 161; Psalm 93, 257 (one verse added); Psalm 94, 562 (one line omitted); Psalm 95, 53; Psalm 96, 629; Psalm 97, 34; Psalm 98, 35.

8 The Psalms and Jesus

Psalm 99, 581 (two lines added); Psalm 100, 491; Psalm 101, 648; Psalm 102, 564; Psalm 103, 339; Psalm 104, 460; Psalm 105, 338; Psalm 106, 354; Psalm 107, 174; Psalm 108 (not used in the liturgy); Psalm 109, 705; Psalm 110, 426; Psalm 111, 650; Psalm 112, 497.

9 Problem Psalms

Psalm 113, 644; Psalm 114, 604; Psalm 115, 550; Psalm 116, 219; Psalm 117, 679; Psalm 118, 277; Psalm 119, 860; Psalm 120 (not used in the liturgy); Psalm 121, 240; Psalm 122, 823; Psalm 123, 1018; Psalm 124, 695; Psalm 125 (not used in the liturgy); Psalm 126, 655.

10 Pilgrim Psalms

Psalm 127, 1033; Psalm 128, 533; Psalm 129 (not used in the liturgy); Psalm 130, 975; Psalm 131, 245; Psalm 132, 522; Psalm 133 (not used in the liturgy); Psalm 134 (not used in the liturgy); Psalm 135, 546; Psalm 136, 605; Psalm 137, 62; Psalm 138, 1055; Psalm 139, 623; Psalm 140 (not used in the liturgy).

11 Timelessness of the Psalms

Psalm 141, 485; Psalm 142 (not used in the liturgy); Psalm 143, 975; Psalm 144, 662; Psalm 145, 353; Psalm 146, 502; Psalm 147, 149; Psalm 148, 944; Psalm 149, 316; Psalm 150, 642.